ON HEAVEN'S DOORSTEP

ANDREA JO RODGERS

D1111792

HARVEST HOUSE PUBLISHERS
EUGENE, OREGON

Cover design by Bryce Williamson

Cover image © by FangXiaNuo / iStock

Names and minor details have been changed in the real-life stories shared in this book to protect the privacy of individuals mentioned.

ON HEAVEN'S DOORSTEP

Copyright © 2018 by Andrea Jo Rodgers
Published by Harvest House Publishers
Eugene, Oregon 97408
www.harvesthousepublishers.com

ISBN 978-0-7369-7163-8 (pbk.)
ISBN 978-0-7369-7164-5 (eBook)

Library of Congress Cataloging-in-Publication Data

Names: Rodgers, Andrea, author.
Title: On heaven's doorstep / Andrea Jo Rodgers.
Description: Eugene, Oregon : Harvest House Publishers, [2018]
Identifiers: LCCN 2017035994 (print) | LCCN 2017051013 (ebook) | ISBN
   9780736971645 (ebook) | ISBN 9780736971638 (pbk.)
Subjects: LCSH: Emergency medical services--Anecdotes. | Emergency medical
   services--Religious aspects. | Emergency medical personnel--United States.
   | BISAC: RELIGION / Christian Life / Inspirational. | RELIGION / Christian
   Life / General.
Classification: LCC RA645.5 (ebook) | LCC RA645.5 .R643 2018 (print) | DDC
   362.18--dc23
LC record available at https://lccn.loc.gov/2017035994

Printed in the United States of America

18 19 20 21 22 23 24 25 26 / VP-SK / 10 9 8 7 6 5 4 3 2 1

This book is dedicated in memory of our beloved niece, Amanda "Dada" Rodgers, who unselfishly put others' needs before her own.

It is also dedicated in memory of my dear friend Lorraine "Lori" McBride, who was one of the kindest, most thoughtful people I have ever had the honor and privilege to know. Her light shines on through her husband, Kerry, and her six wonderful children, Orla, Eden, Erin, Emma, Abby, and Ryan.

Lastly, this book is dedicated in loving memory of my dear friend and fellow first aid squad volunteer, Andrea Raffetto. Andrea's kindness, compassion, and tremendous strength and courage in the face of adversity were a beacon of light to all those who knew her.

....

We wait in hope for the LORD; he is our help and our shield.
In him our hearts rejoice, for we trust in his holy name.
May your unfailing love be with us, LORD,
even as we put our hope in you.

PSALM 33:20-22

Acknowledgments

As I started to think about all the people I would like to thank, it made me realize that I am truly blessed to have such wonderful friends, and that I live in such a terrific, supportive community!

I'd like to thank in a special way the following people:

All the members of my first aid squad, especially Margie Brahn, Judy Cheche, Carlo de Borja, Megan Gepp, and Jack Puleo.

My friends at Fairway Mews, especially Kathleen Walk, Jo Tull, Susan Giampiccolo, Bobbie Clark, and Tedi Makar.

My proofreaders: my husband, Rick; my sister, Thea; and my friends Katy Petersen and Colleen Ehrmann.

Those who helped me to "get the word out" about my first book, *At Heaven's Edge: True Stories of Faith and Rescue*: Gia Beyer, Mary Brabazon and Kelly Westerfield, Sue Domas, Rick and Lynn Height, Rosemarie Korbelak and Patty Faugno, Cathy Cordasco, Matt Magyar, Caren May, Carol Mennie, Father John Morley, Chris Mutch, Loretta Norris, Erin Quinn, Don Brahn, Bob Durna, Lois Rogers, Gretchen Stevens, and Beejay Swetland.

Keith Heilos, for helping with the book dedication for our friend Lori McBride.

Pam Montemurno and Linda Texidor from Coral Harbor Rehabilitation and Health Care Center (Marquis Health Services).

Lisa Mladinich from AmazingCatechists.com.

Danielle Huerer and Lucie Dickenson from Every Voice Educates.

My literary agent, Les Stobbe.

And last but not least, my editors, Kim Moore and Todd Hafer, as well as the entire team at Harvest House Publishers.

Contents

Preface

During times of crisis, many of us turn to the Lord for help. At these moments, the volunteer EMS (emergency medical services) community is blessed to be able to serve as instruments of Jesus. In these frightening times, as we perch on heaven's doorstep, we may unexpectedly find inspiration.

Volunteer Members of the Pine Cove First Aid Squad

Flynn Adams—high school student

Jessie Barnes—optometrist

Dillon Chapman—college student studying to become a high school teacher

Mason Chapman—auto mechanic

Jillian DeMarco—library volunteer

Barry Evans—waiter

Colleen Harper—college student studying to become a speech therapist

Archie Harris—retired state employee

Helen McGuire—nurse

Gary Meyers—college student planning to become a stock broker

Chris Nicholson—computer analyst; also, a volunteer member of the fire department

Ted O'Malley—retired from a career in the national park system

Meg Potter—social worker

Andrea Jo Rodgers (the author)—a thirty-year volunteer reflecting on first aid calls from her early years on the rescue squad; physical therapist

Jose Sanchez—recently retired from a career in politics

Buddy Stone—retired pharmaceutical salesman

Alec Waters—special officer for the police department (summers); college student planning to become a veterinarian

Kevin Wong—graduate student planning to become a psychologist

Members of the Pine Cove Police Department

Officer Jack Endicott

Sergeant Derrick Flint

Dispatcher Jerome Franklin

Officer Vinnie McGovern

Officer Mitchell McNair

Officer Brad Sims

Officer Fred Smith

Paramedics

Rose Anderson

Ty Fleming

William Moore

Paula Pritchard

Kennisha Smythe

Arthur Williamson

1

The Wedding Gift

I will give thanks to you, LORD, with all my heart;
I will tell of all your wonderful deeds.
I will be glad and rejoice in you;
I will sing the praises of your name, O Most High.

PSALM 9:1-2

Honey, I feel lousy," J.J. Fisher said to Cherice, his wife of 50 years. "I'm going to lie down in bed for a bit and see if that helps." From the moment he first opened his eyes that morning, J.J. didn't feel quite right. He thought a bowl of warm oatmeal and a cup of coffee would help, but it didn't. Then he thought some fresh air might do the trick, so he walked their German shepherd, Juno, around the block. Unfortunately, that didn't help much either. In fact, if anything, he felt a little worse. *Maybe I'll lie down for an hour and try to rest.*

"Are you all right, J.J.? What's wrong?" Cherice asked with concern. J.J. and Cherice had been friends since childhood. In high school, their friendship unexpectedly blossomed into love. The dewy-eyed pair got married when they were 21, and J.J. began working in the family shoe business. He had finally retired a year ago, at age 70. Now his son, Geoff, ran the store.

"I don't think last night's dinner is sitting right with me," J.J. answered as he sat down heavily on the edge of his bed. "I'm going to take an antacid pill and put my feet up for a bit."

"Do you think you'll be all right to go to Tiana's wedding?" Cherice asked. Their grandniece Tiana was getting married at the Good Shepherd Church in Pine Cove at one o'clock, with a reception to follow at Pennington Manor.

"Are you kidding? I wouldn't miss it for the world," J.J. responded emphatically. *Family is everything to me. It's the foundation of my life. I love each and every one of them dearly!*

J.J. lay down, closed his eyes, and drifted off into a restless sleep. Two hours later, he awoke when Cherice gently shook his shoulder. His daughter, Jasmine, the spitting-image of his wife, stood next to her. "J.J., I tried to let you rest for as long as possible," Cherice said. "But it's time to get up and get ready for the wedding if you still want to go."

"I'm afraid I'm going to have to pass after all," J.J. said, closing his eyes again. "I'm going to stay home and rest. You go ahead without me."

Cherice and Jasmine immediately grew alarmed. "Now, Dad," Jasmine said, "I know you must feel truly awful to even consider missing Tiana's wedding. The thing is, I don't feel comfortable leaving you here alone like this. I'll make you a deal. Come with us. If you feel at any point that it's too much, I promise to drive you home and stay with you."

J.J. scratched his head indecisively, but then he caught the pleading looks both his wife and his daughter gave him. "Okay, okay. Just give me a few minutes to get dressed." J.J. saw the relief in their eyes. *Family first. If it puts their minds at ease for me to go, then I'll go.*

Although J.J. normally liked to drive, he wasn't feeling up to it today. Instead, Jasmine drove the three of them to the church. Once J.J. stepped through the welcoming doors of the old building, he knew he'd made the right decision to come. *Everything will be fine. I'm surrounded by my family, and it's such a joyous occasion.* The wedding, a beautiful and heartwarming affair, brought tears to his eyes. Tiana looked positively radiant, reminding him of the day when he and Cherice celebrated their own special wedding so many decades ago. *Thank you, Lord, for so many wonderful years. I wish the very same blessing, a wedding gift if you will, for my niece Tiana.*

After the wedding, Jasmine drove the trio across Pine Cove to

Pennington Manor, a banquet hall known for its festive decor and fine cuisine. "Are you feeling any better, Dad?" she asked, gently patting him on the forearm.

"Well, I truly wish I could say I was feeling better, but I just don't feel right. Perhaps the appetizers will help settle my stomach," J.J. answered. He had begun feeling rather queasy toward the end of the ceremony.

"Do you want to go to the hospital? Should we call for an ambulance?" Cherice asked. She placed her hand on J.J.'s forehead to see if it felt warm.

"No, no. It hasn't gotten to that point yet," he answered, reaching for a mini quiche.

"Do you promise to tell us if it does get to that point?" Cherice asked, concerned that her husband might not want to say anything for fear of interrupting the festivities.

"Yes, I promise. Now you girls stop your worrying, and let's enjoy this reception," he said, trying his best to muster up a smile.

The cocktail hour passed quickly. J.J. munched on a bite-size crab cake, but it tasted like sawdust. Next, he sampled a jumbo shrimp, normally one of his favorite things. However, even the shrimp held no appeal for him today. He decided to focus on sipping a glass of ginger ale to calm his upset stomach. *I'm glad it's time to sit down.* He took Cherice's arm, and they slowly made their way to their table. His son, Geoff, and daughter-in-law, Crystal, were already seated, but they quickly stood up as J.J. and Cherice approached.

"Feeling any better, Dad?" Geoff asked, a frown clouding his face. "You look tired."

"I do feel tired right now, son. But I'm going to put it out of my mind and enjoy the afternoon." *I'm not going to let a little fatigue mar this special day.*

After the salad was served, the band began playing a slow number. Normally, J.J. jumped at the chance to dance with his wife. But today his body was simply not up to it. He felt beads of cold sweat erupt on his forehead, and he started getting a tight feeling in his chest. *Are they still playing music? It's getting really hard to hear.* He turned and tapped his wife on the forearm. "Honey, do you remember when I promised I would tell you if I need an ambulance?" he asked, his hand trembling slightly.

"Yes," Cherice replied with alarm. "J.J., what's wrong?"

"Call 911," he replied, before slumping forward in his chair and surrendering to a world of darkness.

....

> **DISPATCHER:** "Request for first aid at Pennington Manor for a 71-year-old male who is unresponsive."

I'd recently finished graduate school and was busy studying for my physical therapy state board licensure exam. I initially joined the first aid squad when I was in high school. (I hate to admit it, but that was 30 years ago.) At that time, I spent summers working as an office clerk at the beach. One hot summer day, a special officer (that is, beach cop) who was a volunteer with the squad convinced me to join. I've been blessed to serve my community ever since. I'm fortunate that I've been able to respond to more than 7,000 first aid and fire calls.

When I heard the tones go off on my pager, I tossed aside my textbooks and rushed out the door. Because Pine Cove is a small town, our volunteers respond to emergency aid calls from our homes. When our pagers are activated by the police dispatcher, we drive to the first aid building to get the ambulance. Our building, which is next door to the police and fire departments, houses three ambulances and has a few meeting rooms. Once we have a crew ready, we proceed to the scene.

Jessie Barnes climbed into the driver's seat and pulled the rig onto the concrete apron in front of our first aid building. Jessie, a dedicated volunteer, tended to answer first aid calls on nights and weekends when he wasn't working his paying job as an optometrist.

Gary Meyers, Flynn Adams, and I piled into the back of the ambulance. Gary was taking business courses in hopes of becoming a stock broker in New York City, but he still managed to find time to answer first aid calls. "Andrea, grab the defibrillator in case we need it," he suggested to me as we pulled up at the scene. "I'll get the suction. Flynn, get the first aid kit. Jessie can bring in the stretcher."

"I'm on it," Flynn said. Flynn, a high school senior, was hoping to go into a career in law enforcement. His mother had told him to go to college first and take some courses in criminal justice to make sure that was what he wanted to do with his life. She also suggested he volunteer with the local rescue squad to gain experience in crisis response.

We grabbed the necessary first aid equipment from the rig and hurried up a light gray stone path to the main entrance of Pennington Manor. A young hostess stood at the front door, pointing anxiously toward the main dining hall. "You'd better hurry," she said urgently. "I heard he collapsed."

We stepped into a crowded dining area. It was obvious that a wedding reception was in full swing. I spotted two police officers kneeling on the ground, close to a large round table by the dance floor. "It looks like they're doing CPR," I said.

"It sure does," Gary said. "Let's get that defibrillator on him right away." At that time, defibrillators, which are used to defibrillate (shock) patients who are in ventricular fibrillation, were new to our squad, and the police department was not yet carrying them. If a patient is in ventricular fibrillation, his heart quivers ineffectively (like a pile of worms), instead of contracting and relaxing as it normally does. Left untreated, ventricular fibrillation, or v-fib, quickly leads to death.

I'd responded to numerous calls in which we'd used the defibrillator, but I'd operated the machine myself only a couple of times.

I spotted our patient lying flat on his back on the navy-blue carpet, his fingertips resting on the wooden dance floor. Many couples stood anxiously close by. Officer Brad Sims was kneeling over the victim and performing vigorous chest compressions. Officer Sims, an imposing figure at six feet three and 220 pounds, had been on our local police department for about five years. Confident and self-assured, I believed he would make a fine police sergeant one day. "We're going to need some suction," he said.

I knelt next to Officer Sims and started preparing the defibrillator. I noticed that a petite woman was kneeling on the other side of the patient, urgently shaking his shoulder. "Dad! Dad, wake up," she said, her voice trembling with emotion. "Please, Dad. Wake up."

Officer Jack Endicott, who was squeezing a bag valve mask (BVM) hooked up to a portable oxygen tank once every five seconds to breathe for the gentleman on the floor, was one of the youngest members of the police department. Passionate about his work, he was following in the footsteps of his father and grandfather before him.

"Our patient is a seventy-one-year-old named J.J. Fisher," he explained. "Family reports that he hasn't been feeling well all day. He collapsed a few minutes ago. We started CPR as soon as we arrived. This is his daughter, Jasmine; his wife, Cherice; and his son, Geoff."

"Please, help him," Cherice whispered softly from where she sat at a table, just a few feet away, tears sliding down her cheeks. Geoff stood behind her, placing his hand on her shoulder to comfort her.

"Is the suction unit ready?" Officer Endicott asked. "I'm starting to have a tough time getting the air in."

"Got it," Gary said, quickly suctioning some debris from Mr. Fisher's airway.

"Much better," Officer Endicott nodded. "It's going in easier now."

I attached the defibrillator electrodes to Mr. Fisher, placing one pad on his upper right chest just below his clavicle, and the other pad on his lower left ribcage.

"I still don't think he's breathing," Jasmine said, looking terrified. She moved closer to her mother. "Oh, Mom, what are we going to do?"

"Pray," I heard Mrs. Fisher whisper to her daughter, grabbing her hand and squeezing it tightly. "We're going to pray."

"Everyone clear," I directed, waving my arm over Mr. Fisher's body to make sure that no one touched the patient lest they also be inadvertently shocked by the defibrillator. Holding my breath, I carefully pressed the analyze button.

"Shock advised," the machine said. This meant that Mr. Fisher's heart must be in ventricular fibrillation (v-fib). The electrical activity of his heart had gone haywire, so his heart could no longer pump blood effectively. If a person is in v-fib, rescuers can try to restart the heart by shocking it with joules of energy from a defibrillator. However, if the person is in asystole (also called "flatline"), his or her heart has no electrical activity at all and so cannot be shocked. If a person is in asystole, paramedics can administer epinephrine (adrenalin) in an effort to either convert the person to a normal heart rhythm or into v-fib, at which point he could be shocked with a defibrillator. Asystole is often irreversible. *People saw Mr. Fisher collapse, so I know it's a witnessed cardiac arrest. That means he has a chance.*

"Everyone clear," I directed once more. I was dimly aware that the bride was standing off to the left side of me, sobbing softly.

"Uncle J.J., please be okay," she cried. "Just wake up and be okay."

The music stopped and the wedding party lapsed into an uneasy silence. I figured that by now, word must have spread through the entire crowd that Mr. Fisher had collapsed. Gingerly, I pressed the defibrillator's red shock button. J.J.'s body jerked in response to the joules of energy that coursed through his chest.

"Check for a pulse," the machine directed.

Gary slid his fingers into the groove along the left side of Mr. Fisher's neck to feel for a pulse. "I have a definite carotid," he said. "Nice and strong!"

I touched Mr. Fisher's wrist to check for a radial pulse. "Good radial too," I said. "Flynn, why don't you try to get a blood pressure on that side."

"J.J. didn't feel well today," Mrs. Fisher said. "In fact, he wasn't going to attend the wedding. He wanted to stay home and sleep, but Jasmine and I talked him into coming with us."

"Good thing you did," Gary said.

If Mr. Fisher had been alone at home, he would not have had such rapid access to defibrillation. Instead, his family may have come home from the wedding to discover that J.J. had passed away in his bed. At least now he had a fighting chance for survival.

"Tiana, dear, please stop crying. It's going to be okay," Mrs. Fisher said kindly to the bride. She stood up and walked over to her. "You know how much your uncle loves family weddings." The two clung together in an embrace of love and hope.

We carefully rolled Mr. Fisher onto a backboard, and then Officers

Sims and Endicott lifted him onto our stretcher. Gary kept squeezing the bag valve mask once every five seconds to ensure that Mr. Fisher received enough oxygen. Although his heart had started beating again, he still wasn't breathing on his own.

"The paramedics aren't available," Jessie said. "I'll radio ahead to the hospital so they know we're coming." Paramedics provide advanced life support (ALS) such as intubating the patient, establishing an intravenous line, and giving life-saving medications such as epinephrine.

That's not good. It sounds like we'll have to transport J.J. without the ALS unit to help us.

I helped Mrs. Fisher climb into the front seat of our ambulance, and then I quickly joined Gary and Flynn in the back of the rig. Flynn was switching the oxygen from the portable tank to the onboard unit while Gary continued to perform rescue breathing. Mr. Fisher remained unresponsive, his frail body motionless on the stretcher.

I sat down on the bench next to Mr. Fisher and peered closely at his face. "I think his color is improving," I said. His previously pale cheeks were now a warm shade of pink.

"I think so too," Gary agreed. "It looks as though he's starting to try to take breaths on his own. Hey, did he just move his foot?"

The three of us looked toward the far end of the stretcher, and I pulled the white cotton blanket up a bit so that we could see Mr. Fisher's feet better. At first…nothing. And then, after a long moment, we saw Mr. Fisher's right ankle wiggle ever so slightly.

"He's definitely starting to move," Flynn said. "It's a great sign!"

A moment later, Mr. Fisher's right arm reached up and began swatting at the bag valve mask. He simultaneously flexed his right hip and knee as much as he could, within the confines of the backboard straps.

I placed my fingers in Mr. Fisher's hand. "Squeeze my hand, Mr. Fisher," I said, and then I held my breath. I wasn't sure, but I thought I felt a gentle squeeze on my hand. "Squeeze it again, Mr. Fisher." This time, there was no mistaking it. He squeezed my hand! *Thank you, Jesus! He just squeezed my hand!*

Suddenly, as if a light turned on within him, Mr. Fisher began taking deep breaths on his own. Gary switched the BVM to a non-rebreather mask. "Open your eyes, Mr. Fisher," Gary said.

I wasn't expecting Mr. Fisher to open his eyes. After all, he'd been clinically dead without a pulse for several minutes before CPR was started. Although he was breathing now, he hadn't taken a breath on his own for at least 25 minutes before that. We'd breathed for him, supplying his brain with oxygen by squeezing the BVM.

To my joyous surprise, J.J.'s eyes flickered open, and he looked at our unfamiliar faces with bewilderment. "What happened?" he asked. "Did I pass out?"

What a great question! What a wonderful, thoughtful question. Mr. Fisher is really thinking. He's making sense. "Yes, you could say that you passed out," I replied. I decided that now was not the best time to tell him that he had been in full-blown cardiac arrest. *There's plenty of time for the doctors and his family to tell him all about that later.*

"That's funny. I don't remember passing out at all. What about Tiana's wedding? Where's my wife?" He tried to turn his head to look for her, but the backboard straps limited him.

"Your wife is in the front seat," Flynn answered. "We're pulling up to the hospital right now, Mr. Fisher."

Things happened quickly when we entered the emergency room. The staff sedated J.J., and then the respiratory therapist intubated him and hooked him up to a ventilator. *I'm afraid Mr. Fisher is going to have to save the rest of his questions for later.*

The next evening, several of our squad members attended a training course at the hospital. After the course, as I was leaving, I spotted Mr. Fisher's son in the main lobby of the hospital and went over to find out how his father was doing. I tapped Geoff on the shoulder, and when he turned around, his face lit up with recognition.

"You're one of the first aid squad members," he said. "I'd like to thank all of you for everything you did for my father."

"How is he?" I asked eagerly, hoping for good news.

"Fantastic!" Geoff replied, radiating with happiness. "He's alert and oriented. The doc is already starting to wean him off the ventilator."

"Wow, that's wonderful news! You made my day!" I said, beaming back at him.

"My father's cardiologist said that without early defibrillation yesterday, he would not have made it."

Thank goodness Mr. Fisher went to the wedding and didn't stay home. It was truly a blessing that he was in the right place at the right time. Through the power of prayer, combined with early defibrillation and CPR, Mr. Fisher would be able to enjoy many more years with his family. *A wedding gift to remember!*

2

All from a Fall out of Bed

I lie down and sleep;
*I wake again, because the L*ORD *sustains me.*

PSALM 3:5

Eloise Marvin rolled onto her left side and gazed sleepily at the alarm clock on her small oak night table. *Four a.m. It seems that the older I get, the harder it is to sleep through the night.* The room seemed unusually dark, making it challenging to see anything clearly. *Darn night-light must have blown out again.*

Eloise had turned 92 a week ago, and her family held a big birthday bash for her at Pennington Manor. She had enjoyed a truly magical day, celebrating with her children, grandchildren, and friends. But, she reflected, she was starting to feel every bit of her 92 years. Last year, she had finally given in and started using a walker with wheels on the front. Her back often bothered her, and she wasn't as steady on her feet as she used to be.

Now that I'm awake, I might as well get a sip of water. Eloise reached across her night table, but the glass was difficult to see and just out of reach. She stretched farther and farther until her fingers gripped the rim of the glass. However, as she tried to roll back onto the bed, she lost her balance and pitched forward instead. Her forehead caught the corner of the night table, and she slammed onto the hardwood floor. Almost immediately, Eloise slipped into unconsciousness.

....

> **DISPATCHER:** "Request for first aid at 617 Shelton Avenue for a fall victim with a head injury."

I looked at my alarm clock and groaned. I couldn't help it. I knew if I went on this call, I wouldn't be able to fall asleep again when I returned home. It's much easier for me to go back to bed if I get home by two or three o'clock. I sighed and slipped on my jeans and sneakers.

Schnitzel, my miniature long-haired dachshund, poked his head out from under the blanket to peek at me. "Stay," I whispered. More than happy to comply, he burrowed back under my covers.

I met up with Alec Waters and Gary Meyers at the squad building. Alec, the energetic leader of our cadet program (for members under the age of 18), convinced me to join the rescue squad in the summer before my senior year of high school. "I'll drive," he said. "Hop in. I heard the police say on the scanner that the patient was initially unconscious, but she's coming around now." He drove a few blocks and pulled up in front of a beige colonial with dark-green shutters. Decorative spotlights lit up the walkway and entrance. A Valentine's Day wreath made of faux red carnations hung slightly askew on the front door. I resisted the urge to reach up and straighten it.

We climbed a steep flight of stairs to the second floor. "It's not going to be fun getting down these steps carrying a backboard," Gary mused.

"We're back here," Officer Vinnie McGovern called to us from one of the rear bedrooms. He possessed the characteristics you wished for in a cop: brains, strength, and courage. We followed the sound of his voice down a short hallway to the second room on the left.

A fragile-looking elderly woman with wavy, short gray hair lay on her left side, wedged between her queen-sized bed and the wall. Her left leg was bent underneath her, and her right leg stuck straight out in front. I could see that a decent-sized egg was already forming on the side of her forehead. "Tight quarters," I said. "But we should be able to squeeze the backboard alongside her."

"I heard a loud thump and came right away," Eloise's daughter, a middle-aged woman named Camille, explained as she buttoned her light-blue floral robe. "I found Mom just like this, but she was unconscious for about three minutes or so."

Alec squeezed in alongside Eloise. She opened her eyes and focused on his face. "Who are you?" she asked, frowning slightly.

"I'm Alec, and this is Gary and Andrea. We're volunteers with the Pine Cove First Aid Squad. We came this morning because we heard that you had a fall."

"Oh, yes, thank you," she said, gripping Alec's hand in her own. Blue veins and sunspots stood out on her milky-white hands and forearms. "In retrospect, I should have skipped trying to reach for that glass of water," she added with a sigh.

Alec checked Eloise over carefully for additional injuries.

"My back smarts a bit, but it usually does," she said ruefully. The skin on Eloise's forehead wasn't broken, so a dressing wasn't necessary. However, we applied a cold pack to control the swelling and a cervical collar to protect her neck.

"Her vitals are good," Alec said. "Heart rate is 90, blood pressure is 104 over 64, and respiratory rate is 14."

I carefully jotted the numbers on our clipboard and then turned to Camille for additional information. "What kind of medical history does your mother have?" I asked.

"Overall, she's really quite healthy. She has arthritis in her back, but we're still able to take a short walk on the boardwalk each morning. She had pneumonia last year, but she made a full recovery."

"Does she take any medications, and do you know if she's allergic to any?" I asked.

"She takes just an occasional ibuprofen for her back pain. She has an appointment with her doctor on Wednesday for a routine check-up. She doesn't have any allergies to medications that I'm aware of."

"Eloise, we're going to put you on a backboard and take you to the hospital to get checked out," Gary said.

"But, honestly, I feel fine," she protested. "Maybe you could just help me get back into my bed."

"I really think you should have a doctor check you over," I said. "That's a pretty good bump on your head." It already seemed a little bit bigger than it was when we first entered the room.

"Mom, you need to go," Camille said firmly. "No arguments. If we leave now, we'll be home before lunch."

"If we don't go at all, we'll still be here for breakfast," Eloise said with a bright smile, but she knew she had already lost the argument. *At least she still has her sense of humor.* "Camille, please bring my book and a couple of magazines so that I have something to read there."

We carefully rolled Eloise onto a backboard and secured the straps. "I'm sorry, but it's not very comfortable," I said.

"Well, now, young lady, that's an understatement," Eloise said with a smile as she squirmed within the confines of the backboard straps. "It feels as if I'm lying on concrete."

"The good news is that it's a short trip to the hospital. And, as your daughter said, hopefully you'll be home by lunch," Alec said in an effort to placate her.

After carefully maneuvering Eloise down the flight of stairs, we placed her on our stretcher and loaded her into the rig.

"I hope my neighbors don't see me," she said. "No reason to make them worry."

Although the trip to the hospital was fairly short, it wasn't smooth. "Sorry about that," I apologized, as we hit a particularly nasty bump. "This road needs to be repaved."

"Don't these things have shock absorbers?" Eloise grumbled. "I'm sorry. Don't mind me. I know you're all just trying to help me. I'm just grumpy because I fell. So, tell me, where do you work?"

"I work at Bakersville Hospital. I'm a physical therapist."

Eloise closed her eyes. "That's nice. I should come see you one day. Maybe you can do something for my back."

"I'd love to," I replied, gently patting her arm. "Anytime."

Maggie, a veteran triage nurse who was always professional and friendly, greeted us at her desk. After Alec gave her our report, she said, "You can put her straight into Room 2." We switched Eloise from our stretcher to the hospital's and said our goodbyes to her and Camille.

"I hope you feel better and that you're home soon," I said, giving her hand a gentle pat.

"From your lips to God's ears," Eloise said with a wink.

....

By the time I got home, it was nearly half past five. Instead of trying to go back to bed, I opted to get an early start on the day. I ate breakfast, showered, walked Schnitzel, and spent the morning housecleaning with my mom. I almost missed my pager going off because of the noisy vacuum.

DISPATCHER: "Request for first aid at 617 Shelton Avenue for an unconscious female."

"Uh-oh," I said to my parents. "I was just there earlier this morning. I hope she's okay."

I knew Gary and Alec had gone to work, but I met up with Dillon Chapman and Colleen Harper at the first aid building. Dillon had recently returned from volunteering overseas as a missionary. He was second cousins with squad member Mason Chapman, and, consequently, they shared the same last name. Colleen, who had mentored me when I was new on the squad, worked as a speech pathologist at a local rehabilitation center. I quickly filled them in about our call for Eloise earlier that day. "I guess she must have been discharged home and took a turn for the worse. I sure hope she's all right. She's a real sweetie."

"Since you already know her, I'll drive so that you can be in the back with her," Dillon said. The three of us headed over to Shelton Avenue. The darkness from the earlier call gave way to sunshine and the promise of a new day.

Camille met us at the front door. "Oh, I'm glad you came," she said, grabbing my forearm. "It's nice to see a familiar face."

"What on earth happened?" I asked. "What did they find at the hospital?"

"Nothing, really. They did a bunch of tests and scans, and everything was negative. We got home about ten o'clock. Mom said she was tired and wanted to take a nap before lunch. I checked on her a half hour ago, and she was sound asleep. I just went back to her room to wake her up for lunch, but I couldn't." Camille choked back a sob. "I can't wake her up." Squeezing my hand tightly, she led us back to Eloise's room on the second floor.

Officer McGovern was off duty, and it was now Officer Sims who stood by Eloise's side, feeling for a pulse. He glanced up as we entered. "Her pulse is pretty weak. She seems to be completely unresponsive to painful stimuli. I tried a sternal rub, and she didn't flinch at all. I just put her on 15 liters of oxygen."

Eloise lay perfectly flat in bed, her cheeks an unnatural shade of white. Her mouth hung slightly open, and her breaths seemed shallow. *Please, Lord, let Eloise be okay.* I performed an assessment, checking her blood pressure, heart rate, pupils, and respiratory rate. Everything was within normal parameters. And yet there she lay, completely oblivious to what was going on around her.

Paramedics Rose Anderson and William Moore, who were both new to our area, arrived within a couple of minutes. Rose had been a paramedic in the Midwest for many years before getting married and relocating to our region. William, a former accountant, had tired of number crunching and switched careers several years ago. Both were knowledgeable, competent, and friendly. Rose hooked Eloise up to the heart monitor, while William started an IV line.

"She could have a bleed going on," William said.

Unfortunately, it made sense. If Eloise had developed a subdural hematoma, it wouldn't have necessarily shown up during earlier tests. If she was now bleeding inside her brain, I knew she needed emergency attention right away. We rolled Eloise onto our collapsible stretcher and quickly carried her downstairs and out to the ambulance. With lights flashing and sirens blaring, we rushed her to Bakersville Hospital.

When we arrived at the triage area, I noticed that Maggie was no longer on duty. Instead, Rose gave our report to a triage nurse named Suzanne. Turning to us, Rose pointed down the hallway and held up two fingers. "Room 2," she said.

We transferred Eloise from our stretcher onto the one in Room 2. But this time, Eloise couldn't hear me when I squeezed her hand and told her that I would keep her in my prayers. I hugged Camille and said, "Please keep us posted. We'll be thinking of you."

I left with a heavy heart. Even if Eloise made it through the day, I knew she probably had a long road ahead of her. I hoped her quality of life would return to what it used to be, and that she could once more enjoy reading her books and magazines and taking short walks on the boardwalk with her daughter.

....

I paused at the threshold to Eloise's room in the intensive care unit. Earlier that morning, I had received physician's orders to perform a physical therapy evaluation and treatment. The diagnosis printed on the order form read "subdural hematoma status post-surgery." I figured Eloise must have undergone emergency neurosurgery immediately after we brought her to the hospital.

My heart clenched at the sight of her. She lay with her eyes closed, completely motionless in her hospital bed. She was hooked up to nasal oxygen, a heart monitor, and multiple intravenous lines. I could see that a large patch of hair had been shaved off the left side of her head, and a bulky dressing covered part of the area.

"Eloise," I said softly, gently tapping her arm. "It's Andrea. I'm here to do your physical therapy evaluation."

Eloise, remaining perfectly still, did not respond. I'd read in her medical chart that she'd remained unresponsive since the brain surgery. *Please wake up. Open your eyes and talk to me.*

Just as I was finishing my evaluation, Camille came to visit.

"I'm so sorry," I said.

"Me too," she replied, and we exchanged a brief hug. "All this from a fall out of bed. It's hard for me to believe."

"She did so well the first time we came to help, so it was shocking to see how quickly she took a turn for the worse," I said, straightening her blanket.

"Our surgeon said things went smoothly during the operation. Now, it's in God's hands," Camille said simply. "Is there anything you can show me that I can do to help?"

"Yes, I'm glad you're here. I'd like to teach you passive range of motion exercises to help keep your mother's joints from tightening up. I also want you to try to stimulate her through as many senses as possible. For example, you can talk to her, play her favorite music, and touch her. If she has a favorite scent or perfume, dab it on a piece of cloth and bring it here. Anything to help rouse her."

I treated Eloise every day for a week. The first four days, I entered her room with high hopes, but she remained unresponsive. But on the fifth day, her eyes were open, and it sounded as if she was humming!

"Eloise?" I asked hopefully. She turned toward me and gave me a whisper of a smile. "Can you squeeze my hand?" I placed my hand in hers. *A definite squeeze!* "One more time, please." *Yes, there it is. Most definitely a squeeze!*

Over the next week, Eloise gradually grew stronger. Soon she could sit on the edge of her bed without assistance. She even began feeding herself. The following Monday, because Eloise no longer needed the specialized care of an ICU, she was transferred to a medical floor. When I went to treat her, Camille was at her bedside. The nursing staff had already lifted Eloise out of bed and into a recliner.

"We're going to try standing up today," I said, smiling brightly. "I think you're ready."

"What wonderful news!" Camille said. "I'm so happy to see this day."

Eloise looked doubtful. "I don't know about this, but I'm willing to try." She slid to the edge of the recliner so that her feet could reach the floor.

I placed a walker in front of her. "On the count of three…"

"I'll do the counting," Eloise said. "One, two, three!" With a big boost, she was up on her feet! She could stand for about 30 seconds before she had to sit down and rest.

A few days later, Eloise was discharged to a rehab facility. I reflected on how blessed I was to witness her incredible recovery.

3

Swimmers in Distress

He reached down from on high and took hold of me;
he drew me out of deep waters.

PSALM 18:16

emember, everybody, hold on tight now!" Larry, a veteran guide
of whitewater expeditions, shouted to us as he artfully weaved his
kayak through the rapids. "We're approaching the most dangerous
point in our trip. Your rafts must pass through a bottleneck between
those two large rocks." He pointed toward several large, ominous-
looking boulders just a short distance ahead. "A lot of injuries occur
here. Let's not let it happen to any of you!"

Apprehensively, I looked ahead and tried not to think about how
narrow the opening between the two rocks appeared. I glanced at my
sister Marie and forced a smile, though it probably looked more like a
grimace. I counted three large yellow rafts in front of us, and six or so
behind us. *Okay, we can do this. Larry makes it look easy. We're going to
be okay. Remember, this is supposed to be fun.*

The day had gotten off to a rough start. Marie and I, along with
our college friends, arrived late at the registration area. By the time it
was my turn to rent a wetsuit, they had only one left. It was much too
big for me and had numerous rips and tears in it, but I was relieved to
have one at all. They were all out of the foot pieces, so I had to settle on
wearing my sneakers. It was a cloudy, chilly April morning, and I didn't

relish the prospect of having cold feet all day. *Well, that's what you get for being late. Perhaps the sun will make an appearance.*

Larry had reviewed whitewater safety rules before we began the trip. Many years earlier, I'd gone tubing down a river with one of my friends and her family. That had been a gentle, relaxing trip without any rapids. We'd spent hours lounging in our inner tubes, enjoying conversation and breathtaking scenery. But as I listened to Larry's instruction, I slowly began to realize that this was going to be a different sort of experience.

"Because it's early spring, we're going to have a challenging adventure today," Larry explained. "The rapids may cause some of you to scream at times, but we'll all be laughing too. The air temperature is 55 degrees, and the water is only about 50. Follow my directions, and make sure to try to stay in the raft."

Larry went on to explain what to do if we were thrown out of the raft. *Mental note: Stay in the raft.*

The first few hours passed quickly. I ignored the fact that the cold water was splashing into the holes in my wetsuit, and that my sneakers were soaked from the puddles in the bottom of the raft. Instead, I focused on the profound splendor all around me. Beautiful tree branches, budding with the promise of spring, arched gracefully over the water's edge. Gorgeous wildflowers, bursting with vibrant colors, bloomed along the banks of the river. A plethora of songbirds chirped their joy that spring was here at last. I soaked in the sights, the scents, and the sounds of nature. I thanked God for letting me enjoy the gift of this special day.

Larry's announcement to "hold on tight" jerked me out of my reverie. Marie caught my look of concern. "We'll be fine," she said. "Just do as Larry says, and we'll pass through this with no problem."

"I know. You're probably right." I was comforted by the knowledge that Marie and I were both good swimmers, and that we were wearing life jackets. *How bad can it be?*

Although I was facing the narrow opening between the rocks head-on, at the last moment, our raft spun 180 degrees. *Oh, great. Now I have to go through the scariest part backwards!* I looked at the line of rafts following us and fervently hoped the one directly behind us wouldn't slam into our raft. As the sound of the rapids roared in my ears, I closed my eyes tight and held on to the handgrips with every fiber of my strength.

Our raft smashed hard against one of the rocks, and then, just as I feared, we were hit equally hard by the raft directly behind us. Almost in slow-motion, I felt my hands slip loose from the handgrips as I did an ungraceful backward somersault out of the raft and landed in the dangerously cold rapids.

Panic consumed me as I felt myself going down, down, down. Or was it up? Or sideways? As I twirled beneath the water, I wasn't sure which way was down and which way was up. *What if I come up and our raft is on top of me and prevents me from reaching the surface? Or what if our raft has already passed by, but the raft behind me blocks me? What if I'm knocked unconscious by a rock?*

The buoyancy of my life jacket propelled me upward, and, mercifully, my head burst through the water's surface. I sucked deep breaths of air into my lungs and silently praised God that I was alive. Frantically, I looked at the raft closest to me to see if it held my sister and friends. The faces I saw were strangers, but one person kindly reached her hand to me to pull me in. Our hands touched, but then her raft swept away in the current without me.

I could hear yelling and screaming around me, and it took only a few seconds to realize that many other rafters had also fallen into the water. *Get a grip on yourself, or you're going to smash headfirst into a rock.* I took a deep breath and recalled Larry's instructions. *Don't try to stand up. Point your feet downstream and float through the rest of the rapids. When the water becomes calm, swim back to your raft.*

Taking a deep breath, I brought my feet out in front of me and used my arms to try to keep my head up as I felt myself being swept along by the powerful current. I winced when I saw another young woman clinging to a boulder, blood oozing from where her head must have hit the large stone. Helpless to assist her, I felt myself surge along. I knew the guide toward the rear of our group would rescue her. Several tense minutes passed. Then, as quickly as the rapids began, they ended.

"Andrea, we're over here!" Marie shouted, waving to attract my attention. I blinked several times and was glad my contact lenses were still in place and not floating somewhere in the river. I quickly swam over to our raft, and Marie and my friends hauled me back in. "Are you okay?" my sister asked. "Where's your shoe?"

I groaned. "Somewhere in the river." I wasn't thrilled by the prospect of a half-mile walk along a rocky dirt road back to our van at the end of the trip. But it could have been a lot worse.

Larry navigated his kayak closer to our raft to check on me. "Wow, your lips are blue. And you're shivering. We're going to need to figure out a way to warm you up when we stop for lunch."

Larry was right. I was shivering hard, and it was becoming difficult to think clearly. My movements felt awkward and clumsy. I knew from my experience as a volunteer emergency medical technician that I was in the early stages of hypothermia.

When we stopped for lunch, Larry gave me his thick sweater to wear underneath my wetsuit top. Slowly, the chill seeped away, and I began to feel much better. Thanks to his thoughtfulness, I warmed up and enjoyed the rest of the trip.

Although I grew up in a shore community, my experience that day reinforced an important life lesson: Respect the incredible power of water and nature. It's a lesson that's been reinforced numerous times through my experiences with my local volunteer first aid and rescue squad.

....

It's been a picture-perfect day, Cliff Bosley reflected as he sprinted across the cool sand toward the ocean. The bright moonlight, which illuminated the large thundering waves, drew him and his friends closer to the water.

"Last one in is a—" Cliff's friend, Josh Jenkins, called out as he dashed toward the ocean.

"Don't even bother finishing that sentence!" Cliff shouted, laughing. "It's not going to be me!"

Cliff, a natural athlete with a muscular physique, easily passed Josh and rushed closer to the surf. *This is the life!* Cliff and Josh, along with their college friends Todd, Zoey, and Becca, had rented a beach house in Pine Cove for the week.

This was Cliff's first trip east of his home in Illinois. He had swum in lakes and pools before, but never in an ocean. So far, he was having an incredibly good time. Yesterday, he and his friends had hung out at the beach and pool during the day and then caught a play at the local theater at night. Today, after spending much of the day hiking at a state park, Todd suggested that they cool off with a midnight dip in the ocean. Everyone quickly agreed.

The five friends paused at the water's edge. "I don't know if this is such a good idea after all," Becca said doubtfully. "It looks much rougher than it did when we swam yesterday."

"I think there's a storm out to sea," Todd explained. "It's kicking up the surf. To be on the safe side, I think we should probably stick close to the shore."

"Good idea," Zoey said. "We'll make it just a quick dip."

"I'm in," Josh said, as he waded into the water. A large wave broke right in front of him, and he ducked beneath the churning white foam.

"Right after you, Josh!" Cliff yelled, chasing his friend into the surf. Todd, Zoey, and Becca followed close behind.

After a minute, Becca turned and headed back to the shore. "It's too rough for me!" she shouted over the thundering surf.

"Me too!" Josh agreed, following Becca out of the waves. "I'm right behind you."

Indecisively, Todd looked at Becca and Josh, and then he glanced back toward Zoey and Cliff. He seemed torn by the knowledge that he wasn't a strong swimmer and he should probably get out too. Just then, a particularly large wave knocked him off balance, throwing him to his knees.

"That's enough for me," he muttered. He pulled himself up and half-walked, half-crawled through the surf and back onto the beach. Josh met Todd halfway and gave him a hand.

Becca, Josh, and Todd sat near the water's edge, watching Zoey and

Cliff goof around in the waves. The moon, which had earlier brightened the water, now passed behind clouds.

"I don't like this," Becca said, standing. "It's too rough, and there's no one else around at this time of night. I can barely even see them. I'm going to tell them to come back in."

"You're right," Josh agreed, also rising to his feet. "They're both good swimmers, but I don't think either of them is used to swimming in the ocean. These waves are getting bigger and rougher by the minute. The tide must be coming in."

"Guys!" Becca shouted, cupping her hands close to her mouth. "Come back in! We want to go home!"

Zoey waved in acknowledgment. "Okay, we're coming!" Fighting the waves, she gradually swam back to the shore and rejoined her friends. "That was fun, but honestly, a bit much." Shivering, she wiped beads of ocean water from her arms and legs.

"Zoey, help!" Cliff shouted. "I can't get back in!" Terror laced his voice. Although he was only about ten yards from the shoreline, it suddenly seemed more like a hundred to him.

Zoey turned to Becca. "I'm going back in to get him." Seeing the worried looks on her friends' faces, she said, "It's going to be okay." She waded back into the rough surf.

"Cliff, hang on. I'm coming to get you!" she shouted. "Where are you? I can't see you. Help me out. Tell me where you are!"

"Zoey, I'm over here! I think I'm caught in a rip current," Cliff answered, his voice shaking. "I'm getting pulled farther and farther out!" *I can't believe this is happening to me. Help me, Lord!*

Todd waded a few feet into the water, uncertain what to do. He knew he wasn't a strong enough swimmer to be of any help. Becca and Josh stood close to him near the water's edge, anxiously waiting for their friends to return.

"I can't see them anymore," Becca said, fighting a rising hysteria. "I don't like this at all. We should never have gone in!"

"Zoey, are you okay?" Josh yelled as loudly as he could as he paced back and forth on the shoreline.

"I'm all right. I see him now. I've almost got him!" Zoey called back, sounding a little out of breath. She reached Cliff and looped one of her arms under his arms and across his chest. "Cliff, it's okay. I'm going to help you," she said. The fact that Cliff was larger than Zoey made it difficult for her to keep him afloat. Slowly, she began towing Cliff toward the shore. However, much to her dismay, Zoey suddenly realized that she too was caught in the rip current. Instead of swimming closer to the shore, she and Cliff were being pulled away.

Now they were both in deep trouble. Zoey's legs began to fatigue, and her arms ached from the effort of holding Cliff's head above the water. She could hear her friends screaming for them, but she no longer had the strength to answer.

. . . .

DISPATCHER to police units: "Request for police at the Hudson Avenue Beach for a report of people screaming."

"I'm just a few blocks away from there," Officer Mitchell McNair radioed into headquarters. Officer McNair, known for his athleticism and quick wit, had been with the Pine Cove Police Department for several years. He pulled up to the scene, jumped out of his patrol car, and raced across the sand. Within a minute, he came upon Becca, Josh, and Todd at the water's edge.

"Please help them!" Becca begged, grabbing Officer McNair's arm. "They're out there somewhere!"

"How many?" Officer McNair asked, gazing out into the darkness. The moon remained hidden behind a cloud, making the churning waters appear almost black.

"Two," Todd replied tersely. "Cliff and Zoey."

"Tap out the first aid and fire department," Officer McNair directed the dispatcher via his portable radio. "We have two in the water!" He handed his radio to Todd, stripped off his gun belt, pulled off his shoes, and, without hesitation, entered the rough surf with a red torpedo buoy. With sure, swift strokes, he swam into the ferocious waves and whistled for Cliff and Zoey, calling out their names. He fervently hoped they would call back to him, helping him to locate them.

When Officer McNair was about 20 yards past the jetty, he heard a feeble cry for help. "Over here," Cliff managed to say.

Officer McNair quickly swam over to Cliff and placed him over the torpedo buoy. Realizing Cliff was too weak to hold on by himself, he helped Cliff hang on to the buoy.

"Zoey's still out there," Cliff said, desperation coloring his voice. "She was trying to save me. We've got to find her!"

Officer McNair continued to whistle and call out to Zoey, but his efforts were met with only a grim silence. It was pitch-dark. Unless Zoey could help him by giving him some indication of her location, it would be almost impossible to find her. Officer McNair continued to search for several minutes, but to no avail. Knowing that Cliff was so exhausted that he wouldn't be able to make it much longer, he made the difficult decision to return Cliff to shore and then swim back for Zoey.

....

DISPATCHER: "Request for the first aid and fire departments at the Hudson Avenue Beach for swimmers in distress."

It was late July, and the surf had been extremely rough all day, with strong rip currents. I jumped into the ambulance with Alec and Helen McGuire. Helen, who worked long hours as a nurse, somehow managed to find time to volunteer for the first aid squad as well. Several more members formed an additional crew and jumped into our second ambulance.

Alec parked the ambulance close to the dunes, near Officer McNair's patrol car at the beach. Helen grabbed our first aid kit. I gathered blankets and flashlights, and Alec carried several torpedo buoys and some rope. As we jogged across the sand toward the water, I could see that the surf conditions had deteriorated markedly since yesterday. Huge waves thundered across the shoreline. A strong wind blew cool air that smelled like rotting fish. Frantic yelling and screaming in the distance sent a distinct chill down my spine. I braced myself for what we might find ahead.

We sprinted the remaining distance across the wet sand toward the ocean's foamy edge. Cold salt water sprayed our faces. Although our squad carried torpedo buoys and ropes, we were not trained to perform ocean rescues, especially in turbulent surf. Rather, our job was to provide first aid once the lifeguards removed the victims from the water. Unfortunately, at one o'clock in the morning, lifeguards were not on duty.

Visibility was extremely poor. I gazed intently into the dark ocean waters, but it was almost impossible to make out anyone or anything. I turned on my flashlight and trained it on the water, but it didn't help much. My gut clenched when I noted that two young men and a young woman were at the water's edge, clutching each other and sobbing. Officer Brad Sims stood a few feet away.

"What have we got?" Alec asked him.

"Two young people are somewhere in the water," Officer Sims replied. "Mitchell went in after them before I got here." I sensed his concern for his fellow officer and the swimmers in distress by the tightness in his fixed jaw as he stared out at the water. "He doesn't have a line on him, and I can't see or hear him."

I knew that if anyone could help rescue the pair, it was Officer McNair. He was a former ocean lifeguard and a tremendous swimmer. But at the same time, I was uneasy, knowing he was attempting the rescue without a safety line attached to him. I realized that he too was now in critical danger. *Dear Lord, please help these two people and keep Officer McNair safe.*

Officer Sims pointed to the three friends huddled close together. "They decided to take a late-night dip. One of them got in trouble, and another went back in to help him. They said the two then disappeared into the darkness."

I grimaced. It was hard to imagine finding anyone in the pitch-black ocean water. *It will take a miracle to save them.* I listened intently, trying to hear any indication that they were still alive. Unfortunately, it was difficult to hear over the sound of the thundering waves as they crashed upon the shore. The fire department, led by Chief Ray Watson, arrived and lit up the scene so that we could see a little better.

I thought back to the day when I flipped out of our raft while whitewater rafting, and I remembered the stark fear I felt in those few moments before I reached safety. My heart went out to the two young people who now faced the same uncertainty.

"I see them!" Officer Sims yelled. "They're coming in!"

My heart lurched with relief. I could just about make out the dim outline of Officer McNair, pulling in one of the victims. Several of our first aid members and firefighters rushed over to help pull them both out of the water.

"I'm going back in," Officer McNair said, determination punctuating his words. "There's still one out there."

By now, word of the crisis had spread, and a few off-duty lifeguards had arrived to help. They efficiently hooked a safety line to Officer McNair. I breathed a sigh of relief. Now we knew he would be safe.

"The coast guard and a few local dive teams are on the way," Officer Sims told him. Officer McNair nodded, and then he bravely returned into the rough ocean waters.

We knelt down next to Cliff, quickly turning him to his side as he began retching up ocean water. Helen placed him on high-flow oxygen, while Alec checked his pulse and blood pressure. I watched with relief as Cliff's ashen face began to gradually regain a normal color. *It's a miracle this young man is alive.* As a team, we strapped Cliff to a backboard so we could carry him across the sand to our ambulance stretcher on the boardwalk. Within minutes, several of our members were transporting him to Bakersville Hospital.

A short time later, a coast guard helicopter arrived. Two dive teams from local towns also came to assist. Unfortunately, the water was so rough and the visibility so poor that the only way a diver could locate someone would be to physically touch him or her. After another 30 minutes or so, Officer McNair, unable to find Zoey, returned to the shore.

We all stood shoulder to shoulder for many hours at the ocean's edge, futilely directing our flashlights into the murky darkness, hoping we would see Zoey's head pop up in the surf. But with each minute that passed, our hopes dimmed. Although the dive teams intensively searched the area, they were unable to locate Zoey. Her heroic decision to go back and rescue her friend Cliff ultimately resulted in the loss of her life.

I was incredibly proud of Officer McNair's heroism. It was truly a blessing from God that he happened to be on duty that night. He was the strongest swimmer on the police department. If he hadn't been working that night, Cliff might also have drowned. Although exhausted and shaken from the near-drowning, Cliff went on to make a complete recovery. Officer McNair won a medal of valor for his life-saving efforts.

4

Just One Beer

You, LORD, hear the desire of the afflicted;
you encourage them, and you listen to their cry.

PSALM 10:17

t feels so good to be home again and out of rehab. That is, if I can call
this home. Stew Davis leaned back and kicked his long legs up onto
a beat-up coffee table. Since he'd been released from rehab a few days
ago, he was living with his fiancée, Wanda Higgins. Wanda was renting a room on the third floor of an old Victorian house that had fallen
into serious disrepair. The wallpaper was peeling, and bare drywall
was peeking out in some places. The gray wall-to-wall carpeting was
threadbare, especially in the hallway connecting the bedroom with
the postage-stamp-sized living room. Stew thought that the place was
pretty much a dump, but it was definitely better than being out on
the street.

This time it's going to be different. This time I'm going to stay away
from booze. It's caused me nothing but heartache. I can be strong. I can
do this. Stew sincerely wanted to make changes in his life. He wasn't
thrilled with the way it had been going ever since he turned 18, when
his parents kicked him out of the house on his birthday. He couldn't
blame them. He'd been a troublemaker since the sixth grade, when he
was suspended for sneaking a cigarette lighter into school and setting
a garbage can on fire. Things went downhill from there. He tangled

with teachers, principals, and the law on a weekly basis. He'd made his mother absolutely miserable, to the point where she and his father simply couldn't take it anymore. So, at the tender age of 18, Stew was out on the street.

But now that he was 25, he was starting to regret all those poor choices he'd made. He wanted to get a job and a real apartment, instead of crashing with his fiancée. Through rehab, he'd realized he would need to abstain from alcohol if he was going to succeed. Liquor was absolute poison to him. *I need to accept that I'm an alcoholic and just stay away from the stuff. Christmas is only three days away. It's a time of rebirth. I'm going to start over again.*

Wanda wandered into the living room and sat down across from Stew on an old sofa that she had found while "Dumpster diving." She held a cold can of beer in one hand and a bowl of pretzels in her other. Placing the beer and pretzels onto the coffee table, next to Stew's feet, she quickly twisted her long brown hair up into a loose bun.

Stew eyed the beer but then sighed and looked away. "Wanda, you know I asked you not to drink in front of me. I'm trying to turn over a new leaf." Nervously, he reached into his pocket for a cigarette, which he quickly lit. He took a few long drags, willing himself to stop thinking about how fantastic that beer would taste right now.

"Oh, Stew, don't tell me you're going to turn into a total bore now that you're finally home. I should be allowed to drink in my own house. Anyway, I'm just going to have one." She cracked open the can and took a long, slow swig.

"For crying out loud, Wanda, it's only ten o'clock in the morning. Give me a break. You can't be starting with that stuff already. You know how hard it is for me to resist." Stew felt himself breaking into a cold sweat. *You can do this. Just walk away. Go into the bedroom. Or go outside and take a walk in the fresh air.*

"Oh, come on. You can have the rest of this one. I'll get another for myself." She pushed the can closer to him.

"No, thanks," Stew said firmly, although mentally he was already lifting the can to his lips. He felt his hand start to tremble, so he sat on it to make it stop.

"No, really," Wanda said. "That one's for you. One beer can't hurt." She stood up, went to the mini fridge, and pulled out another beer.

Stew felt his good intentions begin to crumble. *Okay, just this one beer…*

. . . .

> **DISPATCHER:** "Request for first aid at 1807 Waverly Drive, third floor, for a 25-year-old male with seizures."

I drove past the house on my way to the first aid building but noticed that the police weren't there yet. I couldn't pinpoint why exactly, but something about the place gave me the creeps. To be on the safe side, I decided to go to our building first and then come over with the ambulance. That would give the police a chance to arrive and secure the scene. Jessie Barnes was already in the driver's seat, and Ted O'Malley sat next to him. Ted, an amazing and inspirational member, had originally joined our rescue squad several decades earlier. Last year, he'd retired from his career with the national park system.

Helen and Chris Nicholson joined me in the back of the ambulance. Chris, a computer analyst, was also a volunteer member of the fire department. Because we had a full crew, Jessie notified the dispatcher that we were responding. We drove with lights and sirens to Waverly Drive.

We began to briskly climb several narrow flights of creaky stairs as we made our way toward the third floor. Numerous light fixtures had burned out, making it difficult to see clearly. Despite the relative darkness, I noticed that the grungy yellow wallpaper was peeling off the walls in some spots. The stairwell reeked of stale cigarette smoke and booze.

"Oh, yeah, a nice breath of fresh air in here," Jessie joked.

"I'm afraid I'm going to get drunk on the fumes," Chris replied.

As we approached the third floor, a woman's shrieks suddenly pierced the still air, causing us to hasten our pace.

"Take it up a notch!" Jessie exclaimed, as we quickly followed the sound of the woman's screaming down a dimly lit hallway to the last door on the right. When Jessie thrust the door open, we found Officer Endicott and Officer McGovern performing CPR on a young man who was lying flat on his back in a small, cramped living room.

"His name is Stew Davis. We found him like this and started CPR right away," Officer McGovern said, as he readjusted the position of the bag valve mask. "We hooked him up to the defibrillator, but no shock has been advised so far."

I was struck by the youthful appearance of our patient. *How sad to be doing CPR on such a young guy. I wonder what happened to him. Did he overdose?* The police had already cut off Stew's T-shirt, which revealed his pale, narrow chest. Numerous colorful tattoos adorned his upper arms. A cigarette stub lay on the floor next to his right hand.

"Wow, this looks like a lot more than just a seizure," Chris said. "I'll run back down for the suction just in case we need it."

"Good idea," Helen said. "Please grab the backboard too while you're down there."

Officer Endicott, pausing briefly between a set of chest compressions, pointed toward a young woman, who stood sobbing hysterically just a few feet away. Her arms were wrapped tightly across her chest as if she were trying to squeeze away her agitation. "That's Stew's fiancée, Wanda Higgins. Hopefully, she can give you his info. We don't really have anything yet."

Wanda stared at Stew, almost as if in a trance. "Is he dead? Is he breathing? What are you doing to his chest?" Her own breathing became rapid as her anxiety obviously skyrocketed. She began swaying unsteadily on her feet, and she grabbed a wall to support herself.

I tapped Wanda gently on her shoulder and led her over to the sofa to sit down. "Wanda," I said softly. "Can you tell me about your fiancé? What happened today?"

"This is all my fault," she said, sobbing. "I should never have given him that drink."

"Okay, Wanda, try to take a deep breath and slow down your breathing. What kind of medical history does Stew have?" I asked.

"Stew's an alcoholic. He just got out of rehab again a few days ago. He was trying so hard this morning to resist, but I pushed him until he caved in and had a beer. He meant to have only one, but one led to another."

"How many drinks do you think he's had? What time did you start drinking?" I probed.

"I have no idea how many we've had, but we started drinking at ten o'clock this morning, and we've been drinking all day. Stew fell off the wagon, and it's all my fault!" Filled with regret and self-recrimination, Wanda started sobbing even harder.

"What were you drinking?" I asked, glancing over my shoulder to see how Stew was doing.

"Just beer," Wanda answered, pulling nervously at her eyebrow. "As far as I can remember."

"I'm going to need that suction," Helen said. Chris quickly ran some water through the suction catheter before handing it to her.

"How long has Stew been like this?" I asked.

"Well, he passed out about a half hour ago, but I thought he was okay. He just needed to sleep it off, you know? But then it was so terrible. He started seizing, and he just wouldn't stop." She rose to her feet, swayed unsteadily, and sat back down again.

"How long did the seizure last?" I asked, making notes on our call sheet.

"At least five minutes. Maybe more. When he wouldn't stop seizing, I yelled out the door for someone to call 911. Is he going to die?" Tears coursed down her cheeks, moistening the front of her shirt.

I handed Wanda some tissues and gently patted her shoulder. "We're doing everything we can for Stew."

"Someone turn down the heat in here," Jessie said, sweat dripping from his forehead. "Or open a window."

It was tight quarters in the little living room. Helen tried to open the nearest window, but it was stuck shut from too many layers of old paint. I fanned myself with the call sheet and unzipped my coat. It didn't help much.

"Defibrillator's still saying no shock advised," Ted said. "Continue CPR."

I glanced at my wristwatch. At this point, we'd been working on Stew for about 15 minutes. His chances for resuscitation were slipping away like petals from a rose after an autumn frost. Chris took over chest compressions from Jessie, while Ted now squeezed the bag valve mask once every five seconds. Time ticked by slowly.

"Where are the medics?" I asked Officer Endicott as I briefly paused from filling out the call sheet.

"They should be here any minute. I heard them say on the radio that they got caught up at the bridge."

"It looks like Stew might be trying to take a breath on his own," Helen said.

I noticed that Stew's chest rose and fell in the five-second pause between the breaths he was receiving from the BVM. "Yes, he definitely seems to be making an effort," I agreed, my hopes for a positive outcome beginning to rise.

"Check for a pulse," Ted directed, pausing from squeezing the bag valve mask.

"I think I've got a weak carotid," Jessie said. "Can someone else confirm?"

Helen placed her fingers on the other side of Stew's neck. "Yes, I can feel a pulse. And it's nice and strong now."

Almost miraculously, Stew's dusky gray face gradually turned a healthy pink. His attempts at breathing were more regular now, and Ted worked to assist Stew's ventilations with the bag valve mask.

"Is he breathing? Is Stew breathing on his own now?" Wanda asked, jumping to her feet. "Please tell me that he's breathing on his own. Someone tell me he's going to be okay!" She sank back down onto the sofa and buried her face in her hands. Officer Endicott stood next to her, speaking words of comfort.

We rolled Stew onto his side and placed a backboard underneath him. He began breathing so well that we switched from the bag valve mask to high-flow oxygen via a non-rebreather mask. *You just never know. It looked so grim when we first got here, and I wasn't sure if he had a chance. Now it looks as if Stew is going to make it.*

We transported him to Bakersville Hospital, where he was admitted to the intensive care unit. I reflected that Stew had just received the most precious Christmas gift possible: a second chance at life. Our squad learned that Stew was discharged home a week later. I hoped he would be better able to resist the temptation of alcohol in the future, and that he would learn to live life a little smarter. *Twenty-five is way too young to die!*

5

Dear Old Friends

I call on you, my God, for you will answer me;
turn your ear to me and hear my prayer.
Show me the wonders of your great love,
you who save by your right hand
those who take refuge in you from their foes.

PSALM 17:6-7

Eliza Wheeler and her very dear friend Maurice Key had enjoyed sharing philosophical discussions together over the decades. In fact, many years ago, when they were children, Eliza clearly recalled debating with Maurice whether it was okay to ever step on an ant. Maurice argued passionately on behalf of the ant's rights. It was hardly surprising to Eliza that as an adult, Maurice had become a family physician.

As they grew older, their discussions became more centered on life-and-death issues of humans rather than bugs.

"Maurice, have you ever resuscitated someone and then wondered if you did the right thing? What if it was that person's time? What if it was part of God's plan, and he or she wasn't supposed to be brought back to life?"

"I am but an instrument of God," Maurice answered. "If it's God's design that a person die one day or live to see another, then I think my efforts to help only serve to follow his will, whatever that may be."

"Maurice, one day the time may come when you must make a

decision about me. I trust you to do what is right," Eliza said, clasping his hands in her own.

"A decision about you? What on earth are you talking about?" Maurice asked, a perplexed expression flashing across his face. "Is something wrong?"

Before answering, Eliza fingered the old silver locket that she wore every day. "Not only have you been one of my best friends, but you've also been my doctor for all these years. You can't pretend we're not getting older."

At age 78, Maurice was semiretired. He certainly wasn't taking on any new clients, but he still took care of some longtime patients. He recognized the truth of Eliza's words. They truly were growing old together. "If that day ever comes, Eliza, and I hope it doesn't, then I will simply have to trust the Lord to guide my decisions. I don't even like to think about a time I might be on this earth without you."

"And I don't wish to be without you, either. But as you say, it's up to God. Now, enough of this serious talk. How about a slice of my homemade apple pie?"

....

The persistent sound of the telephone ringing awoke Maurice from a late-afternoon nap. "Hello," he answered groggily, as he fumbled to pick up the receiver.

"Maurice? It's Eliza. Can you come over and check my blood pressure? I don't feel so well. Maybe I'm coming down with something."

Maurice was immediately alert. He was concerned about the breathlessness he detected in Eliza's voice. "I just need to slip on my shoes, and I'll be right over," he said. Grabbing his medical kit, he rushed out his front door. He lived within walking distance of Eliza's house. Within minutes he was ringing her doorbell and jiggling the front doorknob to her yellow clapboard home. It was unlocked, so he slipped inside. He found his dear friend perched on the edge of her floral loveseat, looking decidedly pale. She patted the seat next to her.

"Maurice?" Eliza said, her voice cracking slightly.

"Yes," he replied, fumbling to pull his blood pressure cuff out of his kit.

"Do you remember a few months ago, when I told you that I trust you to do what is right for me?" she asked, gently squeezing his forearm. Her blue eyes, faded with age, stared deeply into his.

"Yes, but—"

"That day has come," Eliza said. She closed her eyes, and her grip on Maurice's forearm relaxed.

"Eliza. Dear, dear Eliza…"

....

DISPATCHER: "Request for first aid at 503 Jefferson Avenue for a seventy-eight-year-old woman not breathing."

"I'm going on a first aid call!" I yelled out to my parents. A couple minutes later, I was whizzing along in the ambulance with Gary Meyers and one of our veteran members, Archie Harris. Archie, a retired state employee, had volunteered with our squad for decades.

DISPATCHER: "Update: Expedite. CPR is in progress."

"Received," Archie replied as he turned off the ambulance's siren. "We're on location now."

Hauling our equipment, we hurried across the front lawn, up the front porch steps, and into the home. Sergeant Flint and Officer Sims were performing CPR on a frail, elderly woman, who lay flat on her back on a maroon Oriental rug. Her pink robe had been pulled open to allow easier access to her chest. "It's a witnessed arrest," Sergeant Flint said as he finished a set of 30 chest compressions. Sergeant Flint had been with the police department for about ten years, and he had recently been promoted due to his strong work ethic and excellent police skills.

A distinguished-looking elderly gentleman knelt on the ground next to the woman. "I'm Dr. Key, and this is Eliza Wheeler. She doesn't have much in the way of medical history. She hasn't been feeling well today. I came over to check on her, and shortly after I arrived, she stopped breathing."

While Gary placed the defibrillator pads on Eliza's chest, I put in an oral airway (a curved, plastic tubular device) to keep her tongue from blocking her trachea (windpipe). Archie took over squeezing the bag valve mask from Sergeant Flint.

"Everybody clear," Gary said. He firmly pressed the defibrillator's shock button.

I placed two fingers on the side of Eliza's neck. "I've got a weak carotid, and she's starting to breathe on her own." Even though Eliza was breathing, the effort was very feeble. We continued using the bag valve mask to assist her and to give her a higher level of oxygen-rich air. *She has a chance to make it.*

Gary placed a blood pressure cuff around Eliza's right upper arm, pumped it up, and then listened closely with a stethoscope as he released the valve. "I can't get a blood pressure," he said. He rechecked Eliza's pulse. "Pulse gone."

I noticed that her breathing had fizzled out too. *Suddenly, it's not looking so promising after all.* My heart sank, and I glanced at Dr. Key. I could tell from the look on his face that his relationship with Eliza went beyond simple patient and doctor. *They're probably old friends as well.*

Turning to the defibrillator, Gary pressed the analyze button again. Once more, he delivered a shock to Eliza. Quickly, I placed my fingers on her wrist to check her pulse. "She has a weak pulse again," I said. Unfortunately, Eliza's pulse remained for only a couple of minutes before it faded out. Yet again, Gary pressed the analyze button and delivered another shock.

"Her pulse is back," Dr. Key said. It felt as if Eliza's life was at the end of a yo-yo string. She was alive, she was dead, she was alive, she was dead, and now she was alive again.

Thirty seconds later, I rechecked her pulse. "No pulse," I said, sighing. Eliza's skin was becoming cool to the touch and somewhat mottled, with an underlying bluish hue. Occasional agonal respirations (gasping breaths often associated with cardiac arrest) escaped from her lips. *It's beginning to look grim.*

Within a few minutes, paramedics Arthur Williamson and Kennisha Smythe arrived from Bakersville Hospital. Both possessed not only excellent medic skills, but good people skills as well. While Kennisha began trying to intubate Eliza, Arthur worked on establishing an IV line.

"Wait. Stop for a minute," Dr. Key said. We all paused and looked at him expectantly. Because he was a physician, he was in charge of the scene. "Eliza has a living will."

"Does she have a DNR?" Arthur asked. A DNR is a "do not resuscitate" order. In this case, for us, it would mean to stop CPR and other life-saving efforts.

"No." Dr. Key answered. He glanced briefly at his pocket watch. "At this point, she first lost her pulse about 20 minutes ago." It was easy to see that he looked torn as to how to proceed. Realistically, Eliza's chance of survival was now close to nil. Yet she clung on, still occasionally breathing on her own.

"Hold chest compressions, no intubation, and no IV or medications," Dr. Key finally said. "I know she wouldn't have wanted that. Just continue with the bag valve mask."

Eric and I exchanged looks. *This is so awkward. I've never been in a position of doing half-hearted resuscitation efforts.* Each time I thought Eliza was "letting go," her pulse would somehow come back again.

"We should put her on a backboard and bring her to the hospital," Kennisha suggested. "We need to get moving."

We gently rolled Eliza onto a backboard. "This is so sad," Gary whispered to me. "It might almost be better if the poor woman just passed away. By now, she's probably brain-dead."

I nodded my head in agreement and glanced at the medic's heart monitor. *Flatline again.* Arthur checked Eliza's carotid pulse. It was absent once more. However, Eliza somehow continued clinging on, occasionally still breathing with agonal respirations. We continued to assist her with the bag valve mask. *At this point, aren't we just prolonging the inevitable?*

After a few more minutes, Dr. Key instructed us to stop assisting with the bag valve mask. "She's gone," he said, his shoulders slumping in defeat. He pointed to a blue floral loveseat by the front bay window. "That was her favorite spot. Would you be so kind as to put her there?" In misery, he slowly turned around and plodded across the room. I figured he needed some privacy. *His dear old friend is gone.*

We lifted Eliza off the floor and carefully placed her on the sofa. I could understand why it had been her favorite seat. It offered a great view of the street, and she could follow all the comings and goings of her neighbors. I stepped back and took one last look at Eliza. *She looks at peace.* True to his word, her dear old friend Dr. Key had taken care of her.

6

Seeking Shelter

God will never forget the needy;
the hope of the afflicted will never perish.

PSALM 9:18

When Linda Richardson heard the front door creak open, she couldn't help but shiver under her covers. The sound of heavy footsteps on the tile floor in the foyer filled the air, and then came a crashing noise. *Arnold must have knocked my flower basket off the end table again.*

Linda turned to her right side and winced as pain shot through her hip from the large bruise she had gotten a few days earlier. She briefly contemplated getting out of bed and locking the bedroom door but ultimately decided against it. *He's been out drinking again. If I lock the door, he'll just break it down.* Linda lay quietly in her bed, listening to the sounds downstairs, dreading when her husband would decide to come up. *If I'm lucky, maybe he'll pass out downstairs on the sofa. But lately I never seem to be that lucky.*

She glanced at the alarm clock on her night table and groaned softly when she realized it was one thirty in the morning. *Dear God, I just need one more week to get it all together. I know it's not safe to stay here. I just need a little time to get everything in order—to get some money and pack a few things.* Linda knew that once she fled to the shelter for battered women, Arnold would most likely go into a rage and destroy anything she left behind.

Linda heard the all-too-familiar tread of Arnold's footsteps on the stairs. She tried to ignore the icy fingers of fear that gripped her chest. *It'll be okay. Just pretend you're asleep.* She pulled her long brown hair across her cheek to obscure her face. The bedroom door swung violently open and hit the wall with a bang. Linda shut her eyes tightly, wishing desperately that she was anywhere else.

"Wake up," Arnold demanded, roughly grabbing Linda's shoulder. "Make me an omelet!" The stench of alcohol emanated from his pores, intertwining with the rancid scent of body odor.

"Arnold, please be reasonable. It's almost two o'clock. I'll make you an omelet in the morning," she offered, as she pulled the covers over her head.

"You'll make it now," he replied, yanking her out of the bed and throwing her to the ground. "I'm hungry."

Stick up for yourself. Just tell him no. You can do it. "Arnold, I'm tired," Linda said, trying not to let her voice tremble. *Who is this man I married? He's a complete stranger to me now. All the love is gone. Now it's just fear and pain, pain, pain.*

"Get up!" he yelled, slurring his words. "Get on your feet, woman!" he shouted as he grabbed the wall to steady himself.

Linda slowly stood. She took a deep breath and reached deep inside herself for courage. *Hold your head high. You can do this.* "No. I will not make you an omelet. I will make you one in the morning. Now, if you will excuse me, I'm going back to sleep." Though her insides were quivering, Linda bravely held her ground. She sat down on the edge of the bed and braced herself for the inevitable.

The first punch caught her square in the jaw. She felt her head snap back from the sheer force. *This is even worse than last time. I need to call for help, or he's going to end up really hurting me.* Linda leaned forward toward her night table and grabbed her cordless phone. She managed to dial only nine and one before Arnold tore the phone out of her hands and threw it across the room. With dismay, she watched as it smashed against the wall, destroying her beloved painting of wild horses grazing in a meadow. *How can I reach the phone now? Will it even work anymore if I can get it? How can I call the police for help?*

Arnold grabbed Linda by her hands and dragged her across the room. She began screaming as loudly as she could, but then her world faded into blackness.

....

Gary Meyers and I were just finishing transporting a man to the emergency room—he had suffered an allergic reaction from eating seafood—when we were dispatched for another call.

> **DISPATCHER:** "Request for first aid at the Kensington Condos for a female fall victim."

"Well, at least we're already up," Gary said as he grabbed a blank call sheet and placed it on top of the clipboard to prepare for the next patient.

"Gee, what a consolation," I replied, mentally chasing away thoughts of my warm, cozy bed.

Dispatcher Jerome Franklin was on the desk that morning. He'd been working for the police department for about ten years and was an intelligent and well-respected member of the force. He was known for being extremely dedicated to his job as well as to the residents of Pine Cove. "Be advised, please remain at your headquarters until the scene is safe," he said to us over the radio.

"What do you think is going on, Gary? It sounds like more than just a simple fall victim."

"I'm not sure. Maybe she threatened to harm herself or someone else." If this was the case, the police department would make sure there were no weapons or other potential sources of danger before allowing us to enter the home.

Helen joined us at the first aid building and climbed into the ambulance. A minute later, Dispatcher Franklin gave us the official go-ahead by the police officers at the scene to proceed to the condo complex. When we arrived, I noticed a streetlight cast long shadows across the front lawn of the condo.

Gary and I stepped through the front door into a dimly lit foyer. As my eyes adjusted, I found our patient, a woman who looked to be in her forties, lying flat on her back on the white tile floor toward the far end of the foyer. A large piece of oak railing lay next to her. I looked up and saw a hunk of railing missing from the second floor above. *She must have fallen through the second-floor railing and landed here.* I wondered if perhaps the wood was rotted. *Is this some sort of freak accident?*

"Hello, my name is Gary, and I'm with the Pine Cove First Aid Squad. What's your name?" he asked, trying to gauge whether our patient was oriented to what was going on.

"Linda. Linda Richardson," she answered, her eyes darting nervously to the left and then the right, obviously frightened of what she might see.

"Linda, can you tell us what happened tonight?" Gary asked as the three of us knelt beside her.

"He pushed me," Linda gasped. "I can't breathe." She clutched the left side of her chest.

"Who pushed you?" I asked, glancing around the room. It was empty. I was startled by her announcement. Having been blessed to grow up in a loving, peaceful home, the thought of another person harming her in this way was shocking to me.

"My husband, Arnold," she whispered. "I'm so scared. Is he gone? Please tell me that he's gone."

"I don't see him," I said. "Perhaps he's with the police officers." *How could someone who vowed to love and honor her do this?*

While I worked to immobilize and protect Linda's neck, Gary placed a high-flow oxygen mask near her mouth. Helen began assessing her and discovered extreme tenderness along several areas of her ribcage. "I think she might have a flail chest," she said.

A flail chest occurs when a person has two or more ribs fractured in two or more places, creating a free-floating segment. A flail chest causes difficulty breathing because it becomes hard for a patient to adequately expand their lungs and chest.

"We'll need to make sure the paramedics were dispatched and get an ETA," Helen added. We all recognized the severity of Linda's condition, and that things could suddenly turn even worse.

"My left ankle hurts something awful," Linda said, moaning. "Can you take a look at it?" She closed her eyes tightly, as if to not only shut out the pain, but also to make the entire situation go away.

Linda's ankle was obviously severely injured, protruding at an awkward angle from the rest of her leg. Helen took a closer look. The skin was torn open, and blood was oozing from the injury. It appeared as if it could be a compound ankle fracture (one in which the broken bone pierces the skin). "They'll do an X-ray at the hospital. We're going to splint it."

"Are you sure he's gone?" Linda asked anxiously, opening her eyes once more.

"As soon as I see one of the police officers, I'll find out what's going on," I promised, gently patting her hand to comfort her.

At that moment, Officer Sims appeared. He must have overheard Linda's question, for he said, "He's gone. He took off in his car, but we have officers from all the surrounding towns looking for him."

"Do you think you'll be able to find him?" Linda asked tentatively.

"Don't worry. We'll find him. You can be sure of it," Officer Sims replied with an air of steadfast determination.

"How did you know to come?" Linda asked, taking a shallow puff of air after every two words.

"Your next-door neighbor heard your screams and dialed 911," Officer Sims said. "She looked out the window and saw your husband driving away."

Gary and Helen bandaged Linda's ankle and splinted it with a pillow. As we began carefully rolling her onto a backboard, paramedics Ty Fleming and Paula Pritchard arrived from the hospital. Ty, a longtime medic, was studying for medical school. Based on the knowledge and skills he displayed in the field, I knew he would make an excellent physician one day. Paula, who was a fairly new medic, was compassionate and smart. They made an excellent team.

"I'm going to start an IV line before we put Linda in the rig," Ty said, pulling the necessary equipment out of his kit.

"Good. I'll go set up in the ambulance and call this in to medical control," Paula replied.

A few minutes later, Helen and I settled Linda into the back of the ambulance, while Gary resumed driving. The police radio in the front of the ambulance was just loud enough that I could hear it in the back of the rig. "We have a line of sight on a car that matches the description of the suspect," I heard a police officer from a neighboring town say. *For Linda's sake, I really hope her husband is in that car.*

"We are now in pursuit of subject heading north on the highway."

We waited with bated breath, hoping they would catch Arnold quickly and without any injuries to the police officers.

Gary proceeded along the highway toward Bakersville Hospital. "I see a lot of police activity ahead," he said. He slowed down as we passed a gas station parking lot. I could see numerous police vehicles with bright flashing lights surrounding a dark-colored SUV. *It looks like they have their man!*

When we arrived at the emergency room, the trauma team met us at the door and escorted us into one of the trauma bays. I knew Linda would receive a battery of tests to check for fractures and internal bleeding, and I was thankful our team had safely delivered her into capable hands.

I was relieved for her sake that the police were arresting Arnold. I hoped it would bring her peace of mind to know he was going behind bars, even if only for a little while. I knew he wouldn't stay in jail forever, but I hoped it would be long enough for Linda to have a chance to heal and figure out a plan of action.

Dear Lord, please keep Linda and other women who are suffering from domestic violence safe and hold them in your loving embrace.

7

The Christmas Stroke

Let all who take refuge in you be glad;
let them ever sing for joy.
Spread your protection over them,
that those who love your name may rejoice in you.

PSALM 5:11

ouis Gilman's eyes slowly opened as he awoke from a deep sleep. Welcoming rays of sunlight filtered through wooden blinds, causing him to blink a few times. He glanced across the king-sized bed and noticed that the other half was already empty. A large maroon comforter was bunched up near the bottom. *Antoinette must have already gone downstairs to start making Christmas breakfast. What would I ever do without her?*

Louis hated jumping out of bed in the morning. He much preferred waking up gradually and reflecting for a few moments with silent prayer. *Thank you, Lord, for the gift of this special day, when we celebrate your birth.* After breakfast, the Gilmans planned to go to church. Later, their children and grandchildren would be coming over to celebrate.

Okay, I guess it's time to get up, even though I'm awfully comfy right now. Louis reached for the glass of water on his night table, but accidentally knocked it onto the floor. *That's funny. My right arm doesn't seem to want to cooperate today. Well, forget the water. I'll have some when I go downstairs. I'll just get up and get a move on.*

Louis tried to roll to his left side, but he couldn't move his right leg. *First my arm, and now my leg.* He tried to squelch his growing concern. *Maybe my leg fell asleep because I slept on it funny.* Although he was 85, he'd always been quite healthy. He didn't need to take any medications, as a lot of his friends did. *Okay, you can do this. Just roll to your side and sit up on the edge of the bed.* But try as he might, he couldn't seem to budge. *Something definitely isn't quite right with me.*

Just then Antoinette entered the room, the morning paper tucked firmly under her arm. "Oh, I'm glad you're awake. I was just coming to wake you up. Merry Christmas, sweetheart." Her smooth, wrinkle-free skin made her appear much younger than her actual age.

"Muwwy Quizmus," Louis replied, a lop-sided smile distorting his face.

Antoinette froze in her tracks. "What did you just say?"

"Muwwy Quizmus," he repeated. *What's wrong with me? Why can't I speak? The words are coming out sounding so odd.*

"My goodness, Louis, what's going on? Are you okay?"

The fear that Louis had been trying to bury deep within now leapt into his eyes. "Twubble moving," he said, using his left hand to point to his right side.

Antoinette, a retired pharmacist, immediately realized that her husband might be having a stroke. "You're going to be okay. I'm calling 911 right now," she said, sitting on the edge of his bed and gently patting his forearm as she reached for the phone on his night table.

....

As my family and I exited Good Shepherd Church, I could hear the first aid siren blowing in the distance. "We'll drop you off at the building," Dad said before I could even ask.

"Thanks. That would be great. I left my pager in the car, so I'm not sure where the call is."

"You'll be a bit overdressed," my mom said with a smile. I was wearing a green holiday dress with black pumps, a far cry from my usual first-aid-call attire. When my family dropped me off at the squad building a minute later, I discovered there were two first aid calls, dispatched simultaneously.

"My crew will take the call for the unresponsive patient at the nursing home," Dillon said, climbing into the driver's seat of one of our ambulances.

"Great. Andrea, Barry, and I will take the call for the person having a stroke," Alec replied. Turning to us, he said, "Hop in."

Barry Evans climbed into the front seat next to Alec. Barry, a college student, was home for the Christmas holidays. Although he was working as many shifts as possible at his job as a waiter at the Coastal Cove restaurant, he still managed to find time to answer first aid calls. I climbed into the back of the ambulance and started assembling some of the equipment we might need, such as the first aid kit, oxygen tank, and call sheet. Before I knew it, we were on the far side of town, pulling in front of a large gray house with black shutters. I peered out the side window and saw we were in front of the Gilman residence. I knew Mr. and Mrs. Gilman and their grandchildren. The Gilmans were always friendly, and they made it a point to make others feel welcome. *I wonder if the call is for Mr. or Mrs. Gilman, or perhaps they have company for the holidays.*

Cheerful garland adorned the front porch railings, and a large Christmas wreath graced the front door. I wiped my feet on a reindeer welcome mat, knocked, and entered a spacious foyer.

"Hello," Alec called out. "First aid is here!"

"We're upstairs," a female voice answered. I recognized the voice as Mrs. Gilman's. We climbed an elegant flight of wooden stairs and found the master bedroom down the hall on the right. Mr. Gilman, looking weak and frightened, seemed to be almost swallowed up by his king-sized bed. Mrs. Gilman, who was sitting on the bed next to him, stood so we could better assess her husband. I could tell from a glance that one side of Mr. Gilman's face was drooping. *It looks as though he may be having a stroke.* Mr. Gilman's eyes lit up with recognition when he spotted me. He tried to smile. *At least that's a good sign.*

"Thank you, folks. We're sorry to take you away from your families on a holiday, but Louis is slurring his words, and he's having trouble moving the right side of his body," Mrs. Gilman said. "I'm concerned he may be having a stroke."

"When did all this start?" Alec asked, passing Barry a blood pressure cuff and stethoscope.

Mrs. Gilman glanced at her watch. "Probably about 15 minutes ago. It's hard to say because he was already like this when I entered the room. It may have begun while he was sleeping."

Barry knelt next to Mr. Gilman and took his blood pressure. "It's up; 180 over 110," he said. I carefully recorded the information on our call sheet. "Heart rate 106 and regular, lungs clear, mild pedal edema," Barry continued. "Right facial droop, right-sided weakness with a weak right hand grip. Sensation appears to be impaired on the right."

Mrs. Gilman remained close by her husband's bedside. I knew that the pair had been married for more than 60 years, and I could clearly see her love for her husband shining in her eyes. "Louis is really quite healthy," she said. "He doesn't have any medical problems, and he doesn't even take any medications."

We carefully moved Mr. Gilman onto our "stair chair," a collapsible chair with wheels, which can be helpful when negotiating stairs. Alec and Barry maneuvered the chair down the staircase. I trailed behind, carrying the rest of our equipment.

"The medics aren't available," Alec said. "We'll go straight to Bakersville Hospital." This was many years before the creation of regional stroke centers. Today, a special stroke team is activated at the hospital while responders are still at the scene of the first aid call.

"I already called our doctor. He said Louis is a direct admit," Mrs. Gilman explained. "You can go through the emergency department, but they already have a room ready for him on Four East. I'm going to drive over in my car and meet you there."

Mr. Gilman held his own on the trip to the hospital. He didn't get any better, but he didn't get any worse either. After we arrived at the emergency department, we checked in with Maggie, the triage nurse. The emergency room was crowded, and she was looking a bit frazzled. "Please take him directly to Four East," she said, pointing down a long hallway toward a set of elevators. "His doctor is waiting there for you."

Alec took the lead, and we headed in the direction Maggie had pointed. Once we reached Four East, we met with his nurse and moved him from the stretcher to his hospital bed. We tried to make him as comfortable as possible, carefully tucking him in and placing pillows behind his head and under his right arm. When we were finished, I gave him a quick hug. "We'll be thinking of you."

Mr. Gilman nodded and waved goodbye with his left arm. As we left, his physician entered the room. I knew he was in good hands.

Later that morning, when we arrived back at our first aid building, we met up with Dillon and the crew from the other call. "How did your patient make out?" I asked.

"We did CPR, but she didn't make it," Dillon answered, as he scrubbed our portable suction unit.

On a happier note, Mr. Gilman was discharged from the hospital five days later. After that, he spent several weeks receiving therapy in a rehab facility. He went on to make a full recovery and enjoyed many more years with his wife, children, and grandchildren.

8

Leave a Light On in Heaven

In peace I will lie down and sleep,
for you alone, LORD,
make me dwell in safety.

PSALM 4:8

Try as she might, Evelyn Dolan couldn't ignore it anymore. Each day, it was getting a little harder to breathe. She had oxygen to use at home, breathing treatments, and an inhaler, but they just weren't cutting it. Lately, she didn't have much of an appetite, either. And even when she was hungry, it was hard to muster the energy to make a meal. *Okay, Evelyn. Now just get up and make a bit of dinner. You need to eat if you want to keep going. Something simple. Just a can of vegetable soup will do the trick.*

Evelyn paused to catch her breath, eased herself out of her plush recliner, and padded across the living room carpet into the kitchen. Her balance wasn't nearly as good as it used to be, so she was especially careful not to trip on her long oxygen line. She'd done that a few months before and was truly fortunate she hadn't broken her hip when she fell.

When Evelyn reached the kitchen, she sat on one of her high-back kitchen stools for a moment to rest. Her eyes traveled around the kitchen, pausing on a ceramic angel statue that had been a present from her husband, Earle, before he had passed away. "An angel for my angel," he'd said the day he had given it to her. *Dear, dear Earle. How I love you to this day.*

Sometimes, Evelyn couldn't believe that 25 years had passed since the night Earle never came home. She remembered it as clearly as if it were yesterday. He'd called her a little after seven to say that he had to work extra late that night to finish up a big project. When a state trooper rang her doorbell at eleven o'clock, she caught the look of sympathy in his eyes and knew instinctively what he was going to say. Taking her by the hand, he'd led her to a chair and proceeded to explain that her husband's car went off the highway and hit a tree. He said Earle didn't suffer, and for that she was grateful. *We had 30 wonderful years together, and I wouldn't trade away a single minute of them.*

Lost in thought, Evelyn slowly rose to her feet and pulled a can of soup from the cupboard. She emptied it into a small saucepan, added some water, and turned the heat on low. *I never did care for microwaves, but I suppose one would make my life easier.* She reached into the refrigerator and pulled out a dinner roll to go with the soup, even though her stomach rebelled at the thought of eating.

The emphysema was starting to take a toll on Evelyn. A few weeks before, she'd suffered a collapsed lung as a complication of the disease and ended up spending three days in the hospital. The first aid crew had come during the night and taken her to the emergency room. Her pulmonologist had said she'd developed emphysema from second-hand smoke. He told her that sometimes people with COPD (chronic obstructive pulmonary disease) get a pneumothorax, a fancy name for collapsed lung. She fervently prayed she would never experience that again.

I wonder if I have another pneumothorax. Why is it getting so hard to breathe? Evelyn stirred her soup with a wooden spoon, waiting for it to bubble. *You know you're just delaying the inevitable. You're going to have to call for the ambulance again.* Just the thought of going back to the hospital filled Evelyn with dread. *It's getting so hard to go on.*

Evelyn sat down with her meal and managed to force down a few mouthfuls before giving up and putting down her spoon. She held out a few more minutes before she reluctantly picked up the phone and called the Pine Cove Police Department. "This is…Evelyn…Dolan," she said, struggling to catch her breath enough to speak. "I'm…I'm having…trouble breathing. I need…an…an ambulance at…95 Bergen Street."

....

My parents and I were just about to start eating an early dinner of spaghetti with meat sauce when our rescue squad was summoned. "Sorry, but I guess I'll be late for dinner," I called out, already halfway out the door. "I'll be back as soon as I can."

My dad sighed. "Why are the calls always at dinner time?" he asked rhetorically.

DISPATCHER: "Request for first aid at 95 Bergen Street for an 80-year-old female with difficulty breathing."

I met Alec Waters and Dillon Chapman at the first aid building. "Let's get moving," Alec said. "I just heard the patrolman tell the dispatcher we need to expedite."

We hustled with lights flashing and sirens wailing to Bergen Street. The dark oak front door was wide open, so we quickly carried our equipment inside. I recognized our patient, Evelyn Dolan, right away. I had ridden in the back of the ambulance with her just a few weeks before when she had a similar episode of difficulty breathing. That time had been bad, but this time she appeared even worse. Sitting, shoulders hunched, on her living room sofa, she looked as though a puff of wind would blow her right over. A handmade yellow-and-white daisy quilt was draped over her narrow shoulders. She was struggling to get air in, despite the high-flow oxygen provided by Officer Flint.

"I'm-having-a-really-hard-time-catching-my-breath," she puffed, her fingers clenching the edges of her quilt.

"Evelyn lives alone," Officer Flint told us. "She's been having difficulty breathing for days, but it suddenly got worse while she was preparing dinner. She tried to hang in there for a few minutes to see if her breathing would get better, but when it didn't, she called for an ambulance."

Dillon, whom I admired for his excellent EMT skills and kind bedside manner, knelt beside Evelyn. "Do you have any medical problems?" he asked.

"Yes, I have emphysema and high blood pressure," Evelyn replied. She fumbled to get a list of medications out of her end table drawer and handed it to Dillon.

I had studied about emphysema in my EMT class. It's one of the diseases that make up COPD (chronic obstructive pulmonary disease). Emphysema damages the alveoli (air sacs) of the lungs, which gradually causes patients to feel short of breath. When a patient with emphysema tries to exhale, the air becomes trapped because the damaged air sacs don't work correctly anymore. This makes it difficult for fresh air to enter the lungs. Lung damage from emphysema is irreversible. Treatment can slow the disease, but it can't cure it.

Dillon checked Evelyn's vital signs. "Blood pressure is 140 over 90, heart rate is 112, and the respiratory rate is 30," he said. "Her breath sounds aren't normal. I hear crackles, like the sound of cellophane being crumpled."

I hooked Evelyn up to our heart monitor. At the time, we frequently used heart monitors, though we weren't trained how to interpret them. Instead, we printed a recording of the heart rhythm and brought it to the hospital for the emergency room physician to analyze. If the paramedics were available to respond to the call, they would switch the patient from our simple three-lead unit to their more sophisticated 12-lead ECG.

After we finished assessing Evelyn, we assisted her onto our stretcher and loaded her into the ambulance. Alec resumed driving, while Dillon and I sat in the back with Evelyn.

"How are you doing?" I asked, noting her pallor and severe shortness of breath. The high-flow oxygen still didn't seem to be helping all that much.

"Not so good, I'm afraid," she huffed, her face glistening with perspiration.

"Where are the medics?" Dillon called up front to Alec. "We need to meet up with them somewhere." We both realized that Evelyn would benefit from advanced life support, such as airway management and medications.

"We'll rendezvous with them in the diner parking lot in about three minutes," Alec responded. "They're coming down from the north."

I fiddled with the non-rebreather oxygen mask strap so that it would lie more comfortably over Evelyn's ear. Suddenly, her eyes searched Dillon's and mine. "Are you believers?" she asked.

I spotted the crucifix that she wore around her neck and knew immediately what she was asking. "Yes," I said simply.

"Absolutely," Dillon added.

"I feel as though God's with me right now," she said, taking hold of my hand. "I'm not afraid if it's my time."

"Oh, please don't talk like that. I really hope it's not your time." I gave Evelyn's hand a squeeze and shot Dillon a worried look.

"It's okay." Evelyn smiled. "I've been fighting for so long, but now I'm ready, child. My husband, Earle, once told me that if he died first, he'd leave a light on in heaven for me."

I felt myself getting choked up. *Maybe Evelyn feels ready, but I'm definitely not ready for her to be ready! And I'm willing to bet that Dillon isn't ready for her to be ready either!*

"I see the medics now," Alec called back to us as he entered the diner's parking lot. I glanced out the side window and saw Ty and Paula pulling their equipment out of their rig. As they stepped inside our ambulance, Dillon quickly explained Evelyn's condition.

As Dillon was speaking, Evelyn squeezed my hand tightly. Then, suddenly, I felt her hand relax. I knew before looking at her face that she had slipped peacefully into cardiac arrest.

I slipped my fingers over her carotid artery at the side of her neck. "She's lost her pulse," I said urgently. "Start CPR." *I can't believe that she's really gone!*

The back of the rig became a frenzy of activity. Dillon began chest compressions while I hooked up the bag valve mask and started providing ventilations. Ty hooked up the defibrillator, but no shock was indicated. Paula quickly intubated Evelyn, while Ty started an IV line.

But it was no use. Despite our best efforts, we were unable to resuscitate Evelyn. I'm a Christian, and I firmly believe in the afterlife. I felt confident that her soul traveled straight to heaven. And yet I still felt incredibly sad and shaken. I took comfort in the fact that she was not alone during her last minutes on earth, and that at least I was holding her hand when she passed on. *Evelyn, I'm glad your husband left a light on in heaven for you.*

9

The Lord's Home

Keep me safe, my God,
for in you I take refuge.

PSALM 16:1

Living in a new country was turning out to be a lot harder than Hernando thought it was going to be. For some reason, he'd imagined life would somehow be easier. Instead, he found himself working much harder than he ever had in his life. Not that he minded, of course. He was incredibly grateful for the opportunity to be able to make money and send it back home to his family. After all, they were counting on him, and he didn't want to let them down.

The problem was that Hernando was tired, homesick, and lonely. At least, those were the excuses he used as he rationalized why it was okay for him to go binge drinking that night. The small part of him that was still aware of what was going on now questioned whether it had been such a good idea.

The steering wheel of Hernando's bicycle wobbled when it hit a curb, and he struggled to regain control. *I need to lie down for a while. I can't pedal this bike for even one more block.* Truth be told, Hernando wasn't exactly sure where he was. He knew he was in the vicinity of the place he had been staying since he arrived here, but it was dark, and he wasn't quite sure how to get there.

He swerved awkwardly around a lamppost and suddenly spotted a

71

wooden bench in the distance. *It'll do. I'll just sleep this off for a bit and find my way home later.*

Hernando's plan fell short by about ten yards. His eyes closed, and his bike tipped over. He landed hard on the brick pavers, and he briefly considered trying to crawl to the bench. Before he could make up his mind, he passed out.

....

Calvin Hodgeworth liked to start his day early. Exceptionally early. His alarm went off at 3:15 each morning. After drinking a mug of piping hot coffee (black with exactly one level teaspoon of sugar), he walked Mugsy, his German short-haired pointer, precisely 1.3 miles. They always took the same route: through the shopping district, around the lake, and past the train station. Calvin wasn't accustomed to seeing other people at that time of the morning. That was part of the reason he liked going out so early. He enjoyed having some quiet time to himself, without interruptions and small talk. He used the time for quiet reflection before his long commute to his office in the city.

Calvin paused and squinted his eyes. In the distance, he saw what looked to be a large lump on the brick sidewalk that led to the train station. As he drew closer, he could see that the "lump" was actually a dark blue bicycle with a young man snoring softly underneath it. "Sir," he said softly. When there was no response, he raised his voice a few notches. "Sir," he repeated. Mugsy sniffed the man's shoulder, and then let out a long, low growl. Pulling back on the leash, Calvin backed away and headed to the pay phone at the train station. He figured he better call the police to help this guy before the first early morning commuters tripped over him.

DISPATCHER: "Request for first aid at the train station for an unconscious male, possibly intoxicated."

My first instinct was to pull my pillow over my ears and try to block out the sound of Dispatcher Franklin's voice. After all, it was around four o'clock in the morning, and I had stayed up late going out to the movies with friends. My desire for more sleep warred with my guilty conscience. My conscience won, and I groaned and rolled out of bed.

When I arrived at the first aid building, Buddy Stone was already in the driver's seat of the ambulance. Ted O'Malley was climbing into the front passenger seat. Buddy had retired from his job as a pharmaceutical salesman a few years ago, and he now devoted much of his free time volunteering with the squad. I scooted into the rear of the rig, slipped on some vinyl gloves, and gathered some equipment that I figured we might need for the call.

"The patient is going to be on the east side of the tracks, about 30 feet north of the station," Dispatcher Franklin advised us over the radio. "Officer McGovern will meet you on the scene."

Buddy pulled up close to the curb, and we hopped out into the warm summer air. A soft breeze whispered in the overhead tree branches, stirring the air just enough to take away the stagnant, oppressive feeling of such a hot day. I figured that thunderstorms would crop up at some point later in the afternoon.

Officer Vinnie McGovern, who was kneeling next to a young man, stood up when we arrived. "He's been out cold since I got here. A man walking his dog called it in. He doesn't have any ID on him. I'm guessing he's around 20 years old. He has a mostly empty bottle of vodka in his backpack, and that's about it."

I knelt next to our patient and cringed at the smell. "Those are some pretty fierce alcohol fumes," I muttered, momentarily rocking back on my heels and holding my breath.

"Yes, it smells like it's coming out of his pores," Ted added, shaking his head.

"The bike was on top of him when I got here," Officer McGovern said. "I don't see any obvious signs of blood or trauma though. Just a small laceration over his left eyebrow."

We carefully assessed the man from head to toe and checked his vital signs. Everything seemed basically okay, but he still wasn't responding. "I guess we better collar and backboard him to be on the safe side," Buddy said, pulling the board out of a side compartment.

Ted used sterile water to wipe clean the man's forehead laceration, and then he placed a small bandage on top of it. As we carefully rolled him onto the backboard, his eyes slowly opened. A look of confusion passed over his face when he realized he was peering up at a bunch of strangers. "You had a fall," I explained. "We're going to take you to the hospital to get checked out."

"Speak little English," he replied. "*No comprende.*"

"What's your name?" Officer McGovern asked.

"Hernando," the man replied. He closed his eyes again, as though ready to drift back to sleep.

"Stay awake, Hernando. Tell us if anything hurts," Ted said.

Hernando tried to shrug, despite having on a cervical collar and being strapped to a backboard. "No insurance," he said, frowning.

The trip to the hospital was uneventful. Hernando drifted off to sleep, and I hoped to do the same as soon as I got back home. I didn't think about him again until about two weeks later, when I was working on the Bakersville Hospital's orthopedic floor as a physical therapist.

....

Sitting in a blue desk chair in the small documentation room on the orthopedic floor, I fingered through my new physical therapy orders. I frowned when I read the order for Lorenzo Montego: "Physical Therapy Evaluate and Treat. Diagnosis: Traumatic Bilateral Above-the-Knee Amputation." *Both legs! How awful. I wonder why?* I finished organizing my orders and pulled Lorenzo's chart from the rack. I could see from the registration that Lorenzo was only 23 years old. I didn't think there was any good age to lose both legs, but 23 seemed so terribly young.

As I read through Lorenzo's chart, I couldn't help but shudder. Apparently, he had gotten drunk and fallen asleep on the railroad tracks. *Of all the places in the whole world to pass out, why on earth did the poor man pass out on a railroad track?* My mind drifted back to when we found Hernando at the train station a few weeks earlier. He might have thought himself unlucky at the time, but his misfortune paled in comparison to that of Lorenzo Montego.

After reviewing the rest of the chart, I stepped into Lorenzo's room to perform his physical therapy evaluation. He was snoozing, but quickly awakened when I tapped his shoulder. "My English is not so good," he apologized.

"Neither is my Spanish," I replied with a smile. A blue hospital gown covered Lorenzo's upper body, and he had a white flannel blanket pulled up to his waist. I couldn't help but notice how flat the covers looked where his legs should have been, and my heart squeezed with sympathy for him.

"I make big mistake," he said, his dark eyes filled with sorrow. "Now I pay for it." I knew it would be only too easy for Lorenzo to slip mentally into a dark place. My goal was to get him to throw himself into his rehabilitation. If he could truly embrace physical reconditioning, perhaps it would help him to begin the mental healing process too.

My coworkers and I worked with Lorenzo twice a day for weeks. We focused on arm strengthening, transferring from bed to chair, and wheelchair training. He faced his challenges with incredible hard work and determination. *It's such a shame that he must pay such a terrible price for a brief lapse in judgment.*

I was starting to feel like we were at the point where Lorenzo belonged in an intense, multidisciplinary rehab setting. However, his discharge plan was complicated by the fact that he had no health insurance. I wasn't even sure if he was in the country legally. It seemed like with every direction we turned, we hit a roadblock.

One day, while Lorenzo and I were working on negotiating curbs with a wheelchair, he suddenly turned to me. "What am I going to do? How can I live like this? How can I ever work again if I can't walk?"

Lorenzo's words hung heavy on my heart. He had voiced out loud what I had worried about for weeks. What would become of him? Our hospital could get him a wheelchair for home, but new prosthetic legs could cost tens of thousands of dollars.

I prayed for guidance to think of a way to help Lorenzo with his predicament. I knew our social work department was trying its best to figure out a solution as well. Unfortunately, it seemed like the odds were stacked against him.

A few days later, I ran into him in the courtyard while I was on my lunch break. We chitchatted for a few moments. Then his face turned solemn. "I wish God could help me," he said.

"Lorenzo, may I ask you if you go to church?"

"Yes, when I was a child, I went to church with my family," he replied, fiddling with the brake on his wheelchair. "I haven't been in several years though."

"Well, I think you should consider going. They could pray for you and with you," I began. "You know, give you a sense of community." I knew that Lorenzo lived about a half hour west of me, and I wasn't familiar with the churches in his area.

"Thank you," he said, a small light of hope flickering in his eyes. "I will ask my friends to find a church close to where we live."

Lorenzo stayed in the hospital for another week before being discharged. He had already been on the orthopedic floor longer than any other patient I've treated. It was time to say goodbye and let him spread his wings. I figured I would probably never see him again, but he would always hold a special place in my heart.

Six months later

Zed Nickerson, our physical therapy aide, burst into the documentation room. "You'll never guess who's here," he said gleefully. "Come and see for yourself!"

I jumped to my feet and stepped into the lobby. There before me was one of the most joyous sights I have ever beheld. Lorenzo was standing before me, smiling. Yes, he was standing—on two prosthetic legs!

As we hugged, he whispered in my ear, "I did what you tell me. I go to church. The people there are so nice. They take me in. They get me new legs."

My eyes welled up with tears. The Lord had lifted Lorenzo and carried him to His very own home, where He knew people would help him. At that moment, my heart swelled with appreciation for God and the many unknown faces in his church that came together to aid Lorenzo. *God is good!*

10

Stuck!

*Listen to my words, L*ORD*,*
consider my lament.
Hear my cry for help,
my King and my God,
for to you I pray.

PSALM 5:1-2

Loretta Stanton smiled lovingly at her niece, Molly, as she watched her deftly dice up several stalks of celery. Loretta and Molly had always been close, but perhaps even more so since her sister, who was Molly's mother, had passed away five years before from breast cancer. Unfortunately, when her sister's cancer was diagnosed, it was already very advanced. She fought a courageous battle, but in the end she had gone to be with the Lord.

Loretta was thrilled when Molly invited her to spend a weekend in Pine Cove, for she'd spent summers there as a child. She recalled their phone conversation from several weeks earlier and smiled. "Gene and I are renting a house at the beach for two weeks. We'd be absolutely delighted if you could join us," Molly had said.

"Are you sure you'd want an old-timer like me there? It's a chance for you and Gene to have a romantic getaway," Loretta replied, not wishing to put a damper on their vacation.

Molly laughed. "We have two whole weeks there, silly. And speaking of romantic getaways, why don't you invite your boyfriend?"

Loretta had felt herself blushing. *Yes, I'm 82 and I have a gentleman friend!* She considered Marvin to be a friend rather than a sweetheart. She'd met him the year before at church during choir practice. Since they were both widowed with free time on their hands, they enjoyed being with each other. Sure, they occasionally exchanged hugs and a few pecks, but for the most part, they were both content to keep their relationship platonic. Loretta had decided to take Molly's advice and invite Marvin to join her for the visit, which he was happy to do.

As Molly chopped vegetables, Loretta said, "I really like the flow of this place. You picked an absolutely beautiful house to rent."

"Yes, with a bit of luck and a great Realtor." Molly smiled, her short red hair catching and reflecting the afternoon sunlight that streamed through the window. "The kitchen was recently remodeled—new countertops, flooring, and appliances. I'd love to do something similar with our home."

"I'm afraid my kitchen remodeling days are over, but I'd like to do something with my downstairs bath. Anyway, I'm sitting here watching you do all the work making dinner. What can I do to help?"

"Well, you could peel this onion and slice these carrots," Molly offered. "That would be a big help. Thanks."

The two worked side by side, content to chat and laugh as they reminisced together. At one point, Loretta laughed so hard that the knife she was using to dice an onion slipped out of her hands. The knife ricocheted off the cutting board and slid into a small spoon, which promptly fell into the kitchen sink and directly into the garbage disposal. "Oh my goodness, I'm so clumsy!" Loretta cried out. "Now look what I've done. How are we ever going to get that spoon out of there?"

"Let me give it a try," Molly said. "I'm sure it will be fine." She attempted to slide her hand past the rubber stopper and into the disposal. "Oh no, my hand is way too big."

"This is my fault," Loretta replied. "Let me give it a try. My hands are a bit smaller." She also tried to slide her hand into the disposal. "Oh, my. This is dreadful. I'm too scared to put my hand down there. Maybe Marvin can help. Marvin!"

Marvin, an energetic 86-year-old, was enjoying a rare nap in the sunroom. "Coming, coming," he said, scrambling to his feet. "What's going on? Where are my favorite gals?"

"We're in the kitchen," Loretta called out. "We need your help right away."

Marvin ambled into the kitchen, pausing to inhale deeply. "What's going on in here? All I know is that it smells awfully good."

"I dropped a spoon down the garbage disposal, and now I can't reach it!" Loretta exclaimed. "We need to get it out of there."

"No worries, sweetie," he replied. "I'll get it." Marvin searched through the drawers until he found a pair of tongs. "This should do the trick."

"Oh, brilliant," Molly said with relief. "Good thinking."

Marvin carefully slid the tongs down into the disposal and reached for the spoon, but no matter how often he tried, it kept slipping. "Well, I'll just slide my hand in," he said finally.

"I think there's a safety mechanism in place to prevent you from doing that," Molly said. "At least, our garbage disposal at home has one."

"Yes, I see that. No problem, though. I know how to disengage it," he replied. Swiftly, he did a bit of maneuvering and then said, "Well, here goes." With a swoosh, he shoved his hand into the garbage disposal. Got it!" he cried out triumphantly. But when he tried to pull his hand back out again, he realized that he couldn't. "My hand is stuck. I can't pull it out!"

"Just take a deep breath, wait a second, and slowly try again," Molly suggested.

"I'm so sorry. This is all my fault," Loretta said. "I feel terrible."

"Don't worry, honey. You didn't shove my hand down the drain. I did that all by myself. Okay, here goes." When he tried to pull his hand out, he started whimpering in pain. "It's cutting into my skin. I think I'm bleeding. It feels like there are razor sharp edges I just can't get past."

"Gene's taking a jog on the boardwalk. Let me give him a call. He'll know what to do," Molly said, pulling her cell phone out of her apron pocket.

"Good idea. I bet he'll think of something," Loretta said, stroking Marvin's shoulders.

A moment later, after hanging up with Gene, Molly said, "Gene's on the way here. He suggested pouring some oil down the drain, so it'll make your hand slippery. Then maybe it'll come out."

"Good idea," Loretta said. "I have some vegetable oil right here." Briskly, she poured a bunch down the drain, hoping that it would drench Marvin's hand within the disposal. Once more, he tried to slide his hand out, but stopped and began howling in pain.

When Gene arrived home, he took one look and said, "I'm calling a plumber." Grabbing the phone book, he searched until he found one that claimed to respond 24 hours a day to emergencies. "Well, if this isn't an emergency, I don't know what is."

"That's smart, Gene. A plumber should have the right tools to get Marvin loose," Molly said. She began clearing everything that she could away from the sink, such as the soap, sponge, and dishwashing liquid, so that it wouldn't be in the plumber's way.

Hunching his shoulders, Marvin said, "I don't want to complain or anything, but this sure is uncomfortable."

A minute later, Gene announced, "Good news. A plumber named Duncan is coming right over to save the day. He should be here within 15 minutes or so."

"I wish I could sit down," Marvin said. "My legs feel a bit tired." Unfortunately, the way his hand was trapped made it impossible for him to sit. He would have to remain standing until his hand came out.

"Hang in there," Molly said. "Soon this will all be just a memory and we can sit down to a nice dinner."

"That sounds wonderful." Marvin sighed as he used his free hand to rub the back of his neck.

"I think I hear the plumber now," Loretta said, rushing toward the front door.

Sure enough, a white van pulled into the driveway. A moment later, a young man carrying a fire-engine red tool kit entered the home. "Howdy, folks," the man said, briefly stroking his beard. He stepped into the kitchen and, catching sight of Marvin's arm, let out a low whistle. "Well, this is a first for me, but don't worry, I bet we can get you free in a jiffy."

"Thank you. What a relief to hear you say that," Loretta murmured. "I'm worried sick."

"Yes, thank you," Marvin grunted. "I can't wait to get loose from here."

Unfortunately, the "jiffy" slowly turned into a half hour, and then an hour. Finally, Duncan shook his head in defeat. "I'm truly sorry, but I don't know what else to try. I think we need to call the police department. Maybe they have an idea of how to help," he suggested.

"Anything, just please get my hand out," Marvin pleaded. "I'm starting to not feel so great," he said, leaning more heavily against the rim of the counter.

Loretta stood close beside him, anxiously alternating between wringing her hands and patting his back. "How about a sip of water?" she asked.

"No thanks," Marvin said. "I'm afraid that if I drink water, then I might have to use the bathroom. I'd rather not go down that road right now."

Gene called the Pine Cove Police Department, and within minutes, Sergeant Flint arrived to help. "Good evening, everyone," he said. "I heard that someone is stuck."

"Yes, please follow me. I'm truly sorry, but I've tried everything I can," Duncan said. "Short of ripping the sink out, I can't seem to get Marvin's hand loose. He's really stuck."

"I guess you tried oil?" Sergeant Flint asked.

"Yup," everyone chorused in reply.

"We also tried cold water, some ice cubes, and lotion. It just won't budge. Whenever he tries to pull it out, the blades cut into his hand," Molly added.

"I'm really getting worried," Loretta said. "Marvin has a heart condition. He's had a few heart attacks, and he had open heart surgery earlier this year. I don't think that all this excitement is good for him, and he said he's not feeling very well. What else can we do at this point?" she asked, her brow furrowing with concern.

"I'm going to ask our dispatcher to tap out the first aid squad," Sergeant Flint said. "Let's have them take a look."

....

> **DISPATCHER:** "Request for first aid at 118 Hanover Road for an elderly man with his hand stuck in a garbage disposal."

"Did that dispatcher just say what I think he said?" my mom asked, overhearing my pager. "I wonder how he did it."

"I don't know," I replied. "I thought they have a safety mechanism, but honestly I'm really not sure."

I'm not what you'd call mechanically inclined, but I grabbed a light jacket and quickly drove over to the first aid building. Numerous other squad members were also pulling up as I arrived.

"Buddy, Mason, Ted, and Colleen, jump in this rig with me. The rest of you can bring over the extrication rig," Alec directed. Our extrication ambulance has rescue tools we use at car accidents. Normally, we don't have to bring those kinds of tools into a person's home. Helen, Barry, Chris, Jose Sanchez, and I piled into the other rig and followed Alec's ambulance to Hanover Road. We pulled up in front of an off-white seashore colonial with green shutters.

Once our squad arrived, we all trooped into the kitchen. Everyone craned their necks to get a glimpse of Marvin's arm. *It's easy to see that this poor gentleman is in a lot of discomfort.*

Sergeant Flint and Marvin's friends quickly explained everything that had transpired over the past two and a half hours. "He's got a history of heart problems, and we're not sure how much longer he can stand up like that, especially being in pain," Loretta said. "It's my fault. I'm the one who dropped the spoon."

"It's not your fault," Marvin said. "I'm sure these people will be able to help," he added, trying his best to sound optimistic. Shifting his weight from his right leg to his left, he turned so that he could get a better look at us. "Do you think you can help?"

"Yes," Alec said decisively. "But I'm afraid we're going to have to cut into your sink to do it."

"We're renting this house," Gene said. "Just do what you need to do, and we can figure out the rest later." He put his arm around Molly's shoulders, and she silently nodded in agreement.

Alec, Barry, and Chris went outside and returned a few minutes later carrying various extrication tools. "We're going to cut a wide berth around your hand, to make sure to keep it safe," Barry explained as he began setting up the tools on the counter.

When the grinding sound of a saw pierced the air, Loretta turned decidedly pale. "I feel woozy," she said, swaying on her feet.

I quickly grabbed her, placing one arm around her waist and the other around her upper arm. "Let's go find a seat," I suggested, leading her to a couch in the living room.

"Thank you," she said. "This is all just so dreadful, like a really bad dream. I think my blood pressure is way up. Maybe you could check it, if you don't mind," she said.

"Of course," I said, pulling a blood pressure cuff out of our first aid kit. "You're right, it is high right now. It's 190 over 100. I think you should stay right here and rest a bit."

"I knew it," Loretta sighed. "Well, I'll feel better once his hand is loose. That noise is dreadful. It's scaring me to death. I hope they don't cut his hand off by accident. They won't, will they?" she asked, her eyes widening in fear at the thought.

"They would never let that happen, so you don't need to worry," I said. "They do a lot of training with those tools. Now, if you don't mind, can I ask you a few questions about Marvin?"

"Of course," Loretta said, leaning back and closing her eyes.

"I know you mentioned that he had two heart attacks and open heart surgery. Is there anything else you can tell me about your friend?" I jotted down his address, date of birth, medications, and the events surrounding the accident as she rattled them off. "Okay, I'm going to go peek and see how they're making out in the kitchen. Just stay here and try to relax. I'll take your blood pressure again in a few minutes."

Just as I stepped back into the kitchen, Marvin's hand came loose.

Loose, that is, except that it was still attached to part of the sink and garbage disposal! Helen quickly pushed a chair behind him, and he gratefully sat down to rest. "Wow, sitting never felt so good," he said with a rueful smile. "Now, if I can just slide my hand out from this position, maybe I won't have to go to the hospital."

We tried elevating his arm and applying icepacks to decrease the swelling. Colleen smoothed on some more oil and lotion, but Marvin's hand wouldn't budge. "Looks like we'll have to take you, sink and all," Alec finally said. "Probably not a bad idea for you to get checked out anyway, after all you've been through."

Marvin nodded in agreement. "Well, at least we're making progress. I'm a lot closer to being free than I was ten minutes ago."

I went back to the living room and filled Loretta in. "And your blood pressure is normal now," I said, after rechecking her pressure.

"Good. I'm feeling a little better. I'm going to grab my pocketbook so I can go with him," she said. She jumped to her feet and scurried upstairs to get her bag.

Jose and Colleen assisted Marvin onto our stretcher and wheeled him outside while Mason and Ted carefully supported his arm and the sink. When Loretta returned from upstairs, I led her to sit in the front seat of the ambulance. "Gene and Molly are going to follow in their car. That way, we'll have a ride home," she explained.

As fate would have it, Marvin's hand did finally come loose from the garbage disposal a few minutes before our ambulance arrived at the hospital. The emergency room staff cleaned Marvin's cuts and abrasions, and he was as good as new. I just can't say the same for the sink!

11

One Cookie

I will give thanks to the LORD because of his righteousness;
I will sing the praises of the name of the LORD Most High.

PSALM 7:17

I t was only half past nine in the morning, but it was already hot and humid. The heavy air and overcast skies hinted of thunderstorms to come. Betty Thompson bustled about in her kitchen, busily preparing for a noon luncheon at her home. She was hosting a meeting for the town's "Save Our Trees" committee, and she wanted everything to run smoothly. The group planned to work from eleven to twelve and then eat lunch together. Several members of the committee had already dropped off dishes and desserts. *I really hope the storms hold off until late afternoon.*

As Betty began slicing a cantaloupe, she felt a gentle tug on her skirt. "Can I help?" a small voice asked.

Betty smiled at her three-year-old daughter, Tasha. "Thank you, sweetie. You can put these napkins on the table for me," she said, carefully handing Tasha a pile of floral napkins.

Tasha, with her bright green eyes and long brown braids, was always eager to help. Betty watched as Tasha plopped the napkins on the edge of the table. "Can I help more?" she asked just as the doorbell rang.

"Stay right here, Tasha. I'm just going to answer the door. I'll be right back." Tasha's watchful eyes trailed after her mother. As soon as her mother left the kitchen, she climbed onto a kitchen stool to peek at the food on the counter. Her eyes lit up with delight when she saw a large plate full of chocolate chip cookies. Hastily, she peeled back the cellophane and picked the one with the most chips. "Cookie," she said softly, just before taking a big bite.

....

DISPATCHER: "Request for first aid at 1005 Chambers Street for a three-year-old with an allergic reaction."

Mason Chapman jumped into the driver's seat of the ambulance while Meg Potter and I stepped into the rear section to begin preparing equipment for the call. When I first joined the rescue squad, Mason was terrific about showing me the ropes. He was an auto mechanic at a local garage and often spent his free time keeping the rigs in good condition.

"If you grab the pedi kit, I'll get the clipboard and oxygen," Meg said. Meg, a children's social worker, was a true asset to our squad on pediatric calls.

"Okay," I replied, lifting the small, orange, pediatric first aid kit out of a cabinet near the side door. "I wonder what the child is allergic to. I hope it's nothing too serious."

"Well, it looks like we're here, so we're about to find out," Meg said, writing the date and time at the top of the call sheet. I looked up to see a cheery, bright-yellow two-story colonial with a detached garage. A child's red tricycle sat in the middle of the front walk, and I quickly lifted it out of the way and placed it on the grass.

Mason rang the doorbell as we stepped inside. "First aid!" he called out.

"We're back here, in the kitchen," Sergeant Flint replied.

Before we reached the kitchen, I could hear a peculiar crowing-type noise. As I rounded the corner, I could see that the strange noise was coming from a small, frightened-looking little girl. An attractive woman in her midthirties, who I figured was the little girl's mother, knelt beside her. "Thank goodness you're here," the woman said. "I'm Betty and this is Tasha. She's highly allergic to peanuts. She's had two reactions in the past, and the second was worse than the first. But this time she didn't have any peanuts, so I'm really not sure what she's reacting to."

"Okay, please tell us exactly what's been happening so far this morning," Meg said, kneeling beside them.

"Well, I stepped out of the kitchen for a minute to answer the door, and when I returned I found her sitting up on the kitchen counter. I noticed that she had cookie crumbs on her lips and hives around her mouth. A few seconds later, Tasha vomited. My friend made chocolate chip cookies for a luncheon that I'm hosting here today. The cellophane was peeled back from the plate of cookies, so I assume that's what she ate." Anxiously, Betty stroked Tasha's head and whispered soothing words in her ear.

Meg placed a pediatric oxygen mask near Tasha's face and checked her pulse. "It's 130," she said. "Do you have an EpiPen?" she asked, as she placed a tiny blood pressure cuff around Tasha's upper arm. At that time, rescue squads were not yet allowed to carry EpiPens. Instead, we relied on the patient having their own or waiting until the paramedics arrived from the hospital.

"Yes," Betty replied. "I'll go get it now. I decided I better call you first. I think I'm in shock that this is happening. I mean, part of me can't believe that she's actually having an allergic reaction. I know she ate a cookie, but my friend assured me that they were peanut-free. Otherwise, I would have put them out of reach."

Tasha's chubby hand pushed at the mask. "Mommy," she said in between wheezes. "Me scared."

The hives were spreading quickly across Tasha's face and upper chest. Meg gently pulled the oxygen mask away from Tasha's face and said, "Please stick out your tongue." *Just as I feared; her tongue is swelling too. If she doesn't get epinephrine soon, her entire airway could swell shut!*

Anaphylaxis occurs when one's body has a sudden, severe, and potentially life-threatening allergic reaction to a substance. A person with anaphylaxis may develop swelling, hives, a drop in blood pressure, and vasodilation (widening) of his or her blood vessels. If the reaction is severe, the person may go into full-blown shock.

"What's the ETA on the medics?" Mason asked, glancing at his wristwatch.

"I think they're about two minutes out," Sergeant Flint replied, striding over to a window in the front of the house to see if the paramedics might be already arriving.

Betty returned to the kitchen, holding Tasha's EpiPen. "I've never used this, but the doctor showed me how," she said. Her terror reflected in her daughter's young eyes.

"Do you remember what to do?" Meg asked.

"Yes. I need to remove the cap and place the end of the EpiPen here," she replied, pointing to the outer part of Tasha's thigh. "Then, I push and hold for ten seconds," Betty said. Though her hand was trembling, she firmly pushed the EpiPen against Tasha's thigh. We all hoped that the EpiPen would work quickly, knowing every second counted.

I could hear the wailing of the paramedics' ambulance in the distance, and I breathed a sigh of relief. Although Tasha had received epinephrine, I knew that the dose would not last forever. Epinephrine buys time for a patient to get to the hospital, but it's not a cure.

Mason gently gathered Tasha into his arms and carried her to the ambulance. I quickly hooked our toddler seat to the cot, and we strapped Tasha in just as paramedics Ty and Paula arrived. I took a close look at Tasha and was relieved to note that the medication seemed to be working. Her wheezing was decreasing, and she was no longer struggling to breathe.

"Good morning, sweetheart," Paula said, smiling warmly. "I'm going to put stickers on your chest," she explained, as she hooked Tasha up to a heart monitor.

A lone tear trickled down Tasha's cheek. "Okay," she whispered.

I reached into one of the side cabinets and pulled out a pink teddy bear for Tasha. "This bear could really use a hug from you," I said, tucking it under her arm.

Tasha smiled and closed her eyes. *The worst is over. Thank you, God, for looking after one of your little ones.*

....

We later found out from Betty that Tasha's doctor felt that her allergic reaction was caused by the fact that peanut butter cookies had been baked on the same cookie sheets as the chocolate chip cookies earlier that same morning. Tasha's doctor surmised that even though the cookie sheets had been cleaned, enough peanut residue found its way into the chocolate chip cookies to cause Tasha to have a reaction.

12

Home for the Holidays

Therefore my heart is glad and my tongue rejoices;
my body also will rest secure,
because you will not abandon me to the realm of the dead,
nor will you let your faithful one see decay.
You make known to me the path of life;
you will fill me with joy in your presence,
with eternal pleasures at your right hand.

PSALM 16:9-11

It was truly a blessed day," Imogene Tanner said, putting down her book for a moment as she turned in bed toward her husband, Burt.

"Yes, it was," Burt agreed. "Having all our family together under one roof is what I love the most about Christmas Day. It's the best present I could ever receive."

"I agree. But I must say, we're up much later than usual tonight, and I'm feeling it in my legs. I'm not used to standing in the kitchen for that long. Of course, the girls really did most of the cooking, but I like to try to help out too." Imogene loved nothing better than to create a new dish, but on holidays, she preferred to stick with family favorites.

"That's what I love about you. We've been married 60 years, and you have as much energy today as the day I met you," Burt said, grabbing hold of her hand. "I wish I had half your energy." At 82, he was starting to feel his age.

"Do you want to watch TV for a few minutes before we go to sleep?" Imogene asked, flipping on the power with the remote control before her husband even had a chance to answer. After so many decades of marriage, she already knew that his answer would be yes.

"Okay, for a few minutes. But, could you do me a favor first?" he asked, rubbing his forehead with his left hand.

"Of course, what would you like?" Imogene asked, putting down the remote and giving Burt her full attention.

"Could you please get me an aspirin?" he asked. "And some water?"

"Sure. Do you have a headache?" she asked with concern. Burt rarely complained about aches and pains.

"I just don't feel that well. Nothing that I can put my finger on, exactly. Maybe I ate too much. I'm sure an aspirin will do the trick. I don't want to make a big deal out of it. The feeling will pass quickly, I hope."

"I'll get one right away," Imogene said worriedly, returning a moment later with a pill and a glass of water. "Perhaps you had too much excitement today. Maybe you should see the doctor tomorrow. I wonder if she even has office hours the day after Christmas. Or do you think I should call for an ambulance?"

"No, let's give the aspirin a chance to work first," Burt decided. "Maybe I just need to put my legs up for a few minutes and relax. Watching TV will take my mind off it."

The couple watched television for about 15 minutes, but Burt didn't feel any better. "I hate to say it, Imogene, but I guess you better call 911," he said reluctantly. "I'd much rather be home for the holidays than lying in some emergency room, but something just doesn't feel right. I guess it would be better to play it safe and get checked out."

....

DISPATCHER: "Request for first aid at 410 Cherry Blossom Road for an 82-year-old male who is not feeling well."

I had stayed up later than usual, reluctant to say goodbye to Christmas Day. When my pager went off, I threw on a heavy coat and met up with Barry, Ted, and Archie at the first aid building.

"I'll drive," Archie said. "Let's go!" Archie was always good about getting us organized and on the road quickly.

We jumped into the back of the ambulance and gathered some of the equipment we thought we might need. "I was just about to hit the hay," Ted said. "Did you have a nice Christmas?"

"Wonderful," Barry said. "Couldn't have been a better day."

"Yes, it was a great day," I agreed. Silently, I wondered if this patient had waited, trying to put off calling for help until tomorrow. In my experience, people often delay calling 911 until the holiday is over. To spend your holiday lying on a stretcher in the emergency room is not an attractive option to most.

An elderly woman wearing a pink housecoat met us at the front door. "Hi, I'm Imogene Tanner," she said. "My husband, Burt, hasn't been feeling well for the past hour or so. I gave him an aspirin, but it didn't help. Just a couple of minutes ago, he started complaining of chest pain. Please, follow me." She led us through a small entrance foyer and up a steep flight of stairs to the master bedroom.

We found Burt Tanner sitting up in bed, holding a large basin close to his chest. Although it was obvious that he wasn't feeling well, he smiled to welcome us. "Sorry to get you folks out of bed."

"That's what we're here for," Barry said. "I see that you're holding a basin. Are you feeling nauseated?"

"Yes. I starting feeling like something wasn't quite right about an hour earlier. Just a few minutes ago, I started feeling tightness," Burt said, pointing to the center of his chest. "It hurts right here, and it's getting sort of hard to breathe."

Officer McGovern had already placed Burt on high-flow oxygen, but it didn't seem to be helping much. "His respiratory rate is 22 and shallow," I murmured to Ted, who was writing up the call sheet. "Blood pressure is 196 over 104, and his pulse is 106 and irregular." I noticed that Burt closed his eyes while I performed my assessment.

Just then, paramedics Arthur and Kennisha arrived. "What have we got?" Kennisha asked, placing her advanced life support bag down close to Burt's bed. Archie quickly filled them in on Burt's condition.

"I'm going to hook you up to a heart monitor, sir," Arthur said as he prepared to apply a 12-lead ECG. After studying the tracing, he said, "I think we should take you to the hospital to get checked out, okay?"

"If you say so," Burt said. "I was hoping you would say everything looked great and that I could stay home. Wishful thinking on my part, I suppose."

"Sorry, I really wish I could say that. But since you're not feeling well, it would be better to have the emergency room physician take a closer look at you," Arthur replied.

Burt sighed. "I understand. I was just hoping." Once again, he closed his eyes as if wishing he were somewhere else.

"We've been married for 60 years, and we've never been apart for a single night, except when I gave birth to our children," Imogene said. "I really hope that he's going to be okay and that he doesn't need to be admitted." Her brow furrowed with concern.

"Mr. Tanner, has anyone ever told you that you don't have the greatest veins?" Kennisha asked, as she began trying to start an intravenous line. "They collapse really easily."

"Yes, so I've been told when I used to donate blood," Burt said. "I guess my body is trying to say I should hold on to my blood," he joked.

What a kind, pleasant gentleman. I'm so sorry he and his wife have to go through this. As Kennisha was securing the IV line, I glanced around Burt and Imogene's bedroom. Family photos graced the dresser and walls. It seemed the couple was blessed with several children and numerous grandchildren.

Once Arthur and Kennisha were done stabilizing Burt, we loaded him onto our stretcher and rolled him down a long, dark driveway toward the ambulance. Bare oak branches danced overhead in the breeze, as if to point the way. Mrs. Tanner walked beside us, holding on to Archie's arm for support. We paused before lifting the stretcher into the ambulance.

"Mrs. Tanner, would you like to ride with us to the ER?" Archie asked. "You can sit in the front seat next to me."

"No, thank you. I'd rather take my own car so I have a ride home," she replied. "I'd hate to wake up our children at this time of night."

I hoped Mrs. Tanner was safe to drive. Sometimes, I'm concerned that family members may be distracted drivers because they're so worried about what's happening in the back of our ambulance. Or they may follow behind the ambulance too closely, trying to rush through red lights to keep up with us.

Mrs. Tanner gave her husband a loving kiss on the cheek. "I'm going back inside for a moment to get dressed. I'll meet you at the hospital in about 20 minutes," she said tenderly.

"I'll be counting the minutes," Burt said. "Be safe and know that I love you."

With that, we lifted Burt into our rig. Archie climbed into the driver's seat, and Barry drove the medics' rig. I hopped into the back with Ted, Arthur, and Kennisha.

"Thanks again for coming so quickly," Burt said to us. "I truly hate to bring you all out on Christmas night."

"No thanks necessary," I said. "Just feel better. We were done celebrating anyway, so there's no need to worry." Trying to make small talk and take Burt's mind off his troubles, I added, "Judging from the photos in your bedroom, it looks like you have lots of family."

Burt perked up right away. "Three children and eight grandchildren," he said proudly. "One of my grandchildren is even named after me."

"That's wonderful," I replied. "Did you get to see them today?"

"Oh, yes. Everyone came over. It was simply terrific," he said, a brief smile hovering on his lips. However, as we drew closer to Bakersville Hospital, Burt became paler and his breathing more labored. He tightly clutched the yellow emesis basin in his lap with one hand, and held on to the stretcher handrail with the other.

"Mr. Tanner, how's that chest pain?" Arthur asked. "Are you ready for another nitro pill?"

"The pain's getting worse," Burt replied. "Yes, I guess you could give me another pill, thanks. Maybe that'll help." A fine sheen of sweat glistened on Burt's forehead and upper lip.

Kennisha pushed some more medications through Burt's IV while Arthur slipped another nitroglycerin pill under Burt's tongue. "This will slowly dissolve, just like the first one," Arthur said. "Do me a favor, Andrea. Get me another blood pressure on your side."

I inflated the cuff on Burt's right arm. "It's 170 over 94." It had come down a bit from the initial blood pressure reading, possibly due to the first nitro pill.

Burt drained of all color until his face appeared almost stark white. "I don't think I'm going to make it," he managed to say. "Tell Imogene that I…" Burt wasn't able to finish his sentence before slipping into unconsciousness. Mentally, I finished the sentence for him. *Tell Imogene that I love her.*

Within a mere second or two, Burt stopped breathing and lost his pulse. He was in full-blown cardiac arrest. The unexpectedness of it was startling. *His poor wife! She's going to have a terrible shock when she arrives at the hospital. Dear Lord, please let us resuscitate him quickly.*

Arthur applied defibrillator pads to Burt's chest. Defibrillation is most successful if done quickly. I knew that since it was a witnessed arrest that Burt had a decent chance. There had been no "down time" at all.

"He's in v-fib," Arthur said. "Everyone clear the patient." Placing the paddles down on the pads, he proceeded to shock Burt's heart. "Check for a pulse," he directed.

I held my breath as Kennisha felt for a carotid pulse. "I've got nothing."

We're going to lose him. The shock didn't work. I quickly began to perform chest compressions while Kennisha intubated Burt. Ted held on to my waist so I wouldn't lose my balance as the ambulance continued toward the hospital.

Our team worked to the best of our ability to resuscitate Burt, giving it our all. But in the end, it was no use. We never regained a pulse. Burt passed quickly and quietly from this world into the afterlife.

If it were up to me, we would resuscitate every patient who went into cardiac arrest. But then I remind myself that God has a plan for each of us. Perhaps Burt had finished what was expected of him during his time on earth. *Maybe God was calling him toward the light. Maybe it was simply his time.*

Imogene's gentle voice rang in my thoughts: "We've been married for 60 years."

I imagine it doesn't feel nearly long enough to her.

13

The Rig Runner

*Do not conform to the pattern of this world, but be
transformed by the renewing of your mind. Then
you will be able to test and approve what God's
will is—his good, pleasing and perfect will.*

ROMANS 12:2-3

'll be there in just a few more miles. They'll help me. Samantha Ford
shifted in her seat and turned off the car radio. The voices were beginning to grate on her nerves. She preferred silence.

The highway signs confused Samantha. *Is this the right exit? It looks
sort of familiar, but I don't know…* She flipped on her blinker and took
the exit. *Maybe it will look more familiar when I'm off the highway and
on local roads.* Nervously, she lit a cigarette and took a deep drag. *Okay,
that's better. I can think a little more clearly now. Or can I? Everything
seems sort of out of focus.*

Almost in a trancelike state, Samantha drove on. *Bartholomew Road.
I think that's it. I made it.*

....

> **DISPATCHER:** "Request for first aid at 713 Bartholomew Road for a
> woman not feeling well."

It was a hot summer evening with just a whisper of a dry west wind, the kind of evening when it's way too warm to do much except relax in the air conditioning with a frosty lemonade or iced tea. Or maybe to enjoy a double scoop of vanilla ice cream with fudge sauce and whipped cream. Gary, Mason, Buddy Stone, and I left our air conditioners behind to answer the first aid call.

As soon as we hopped in the back of the ambulance, Gary cranked the air conditioning. Unfortunately, warm air blew from the vents. "Great, this will make for a pleasant call," he said, rolling his eyes.

"I'll look at it when we get back," Mason said. "Maybe we're low on coolant."

I fanned myself with the call sheet. It didn't help much, and I felt beads of sweat start to trickle down the back of my neck. As we pulled up in front of a small yellow bungalow, I noticed that Helen McGuire was already at the scene. About a half dozen people were milling around on the sidewalk near her, and Officers Endicott and Sims were speaking to them.

I studied the people clustered around Helen and the officers. Two men, who looked to be in their mid-forties or so, were wearing cut-off jeans with no shirts. One was skinny with numerous tattoos on his chest. The other was overweight, his stomach sagging heavily over the top of his shorts. Three women, sporting brightly colored tank tops, short-shorts, and high heels, stood with them.

Officer Sims stepped off the curb to the side of the roadway. "Why did you call us here tonight?" he calmly asked them.

The man with the tattoos stepped forward. He removed his old, faded baseball cap, scratched the top of his balding head, and then pointed toward a woman who was sitting a few yards away on the curb. "I dunno. She doesn't seem quite right tonight," he offered, shrugging his shoulders.

"Who is she and who are you?" Officer Sims asked.

"I'm Mac. That's Samantha," he replied, placing his baseball cap firmly back on his head.

Trying to get information out of Mac felt like pulling teeth. Officer Sims shifted back and forth on his feet and then leaned in closer to Mac. "Samantha who?"

"Samantha Ford," one of the women answered.

"And who are you?" Officer Sims asked, pulling out his notebook.

"Gina," she replied, twisting her long, bleached-blond hair slowly around her index finger.

Samantha sat close by on the curb, puffing on a cigarette. Her long brown hair had some gray streaks and was tied back in a loose ponytail. I noted that the years had not been kind to her. She looked as if she had experienced too much of everything in life: too much sun, too much booze, too much smoking. Her artificial nails were chipped and broken.

"What doesn't seem right about her to you? Does she live here?" Officer Endicott asked.

"No, she don't live here," Gina said. "She rang our doorbell out of the blue a half hour ago. We wasn't expecting her."

"She lives in Tennessee," Mac added. "She told us she drove straight here. Not sure why."

"How do you know Samantha? Is she a friend? A relative?" Officer Sims asked.

"She's an old friend," Gina said, nervously tapping a long red fingernail on the side of her chin. "But none of us have seen her in years."

Gary crouched near Samantha. "Hello, I'm Gary. I'm an EMT with the first aid squad. I heard that you might not be feeling so well tonight. Can you tell us what's wrong?"

Samantha stared at her toes, either oblivious to Gary's question or not wishing to reply.

"Do you have any medical problems?" Gary asked. "Diabetes? Low blood sugar? Have you eaten today?"

Samantha remained silent, picking up a stick and scratching a circle in the dirt with it.

I turned to her friends. "Do you know anything about her medical history?" I asked. *Perhaps something from Samantha's past could help explain her current condition.*

They all shook their heads. "Not that I can remember," Mac said, shaking his head.

"I don't think so," Gina agreed, pausing to blow a large, pink bubble with her gum. "But she sure don't seem right tonight."

I didn't have a whole lot to write down on our call sheet. Samantha wouldn't provide her address in Tennessee, so we wrote down the address of her friends. I jotted down her blood pressure and pulse, which were normal. Sullenly, Samantha denied any complaints. *Her friends are right about one thing; she sure doesn't seem quite right.*

Buddy and Gary walked Samantha arm-in-arm to the ambulance and helped her to step inside. Then we strapped her onto the stretcher with two lap-style seatbelts. Mason took the driver's seat. "Let me know when you're ready to go," he called back to us.

I glanced out the ambulance window. Helen had driven directly to the scene, so she was now heading back to her car, opting to stay in town in case there was another first aid call. Officers Endicott and Sims were pulling away in their patrol cars. Mac, Gina, and the rest of Samantha's friends were slowly ambling back toward their bungalow.

Gary, Buddy, and I settled into our seats. "We're all set, Mason," Buddy said. I heard our rig shift into gear, and we began our trip to the hospital. I looked down to buckle my seatbelt, briefly taking my eyes off Samantha. It all happened in a flash. One second, Samantha was safely buckled into our stretcher. The next, she had unbuckled herself and was jumping out the back doors of our moving ambulance! In that brief second, I imagined Samantha landing hard on the road and then getting run over by a car. If she got hurt, I would feel like it was our fault. *We need to stop her!*

Fortunately, the rig was moving slowly at the time. Samantha did not land hard on the ground, nor did she get run over, as I had feared. Instead, Samantha landed firmly on both feet and took off like an Olympic sprinter, racing along the asphalt road in the direction of her friends' cottage.

"STOP THE RIG!" Gary shouted to Mason.

Mason slammed on the brakes, and the rig jerked to a halt. I grabbed the overhead bar to avoid falling over. "Call the police to come back and help us!" I yelled as Gary, Buddy, and I jumped out after Samantha. As I was jumping, I could hear Mason radioing to headquarters: "We need help—we've got a runner!"

We raced down the street after Samantha. I was glad that I ran track in high school! Helen, who hadn't quite reached her car yet, rushed over to help. Officers Sims and Endicott, who had only driven around the corner, immediately returned to assist us as well. Samantha finally came to a stop in front of her friends' bungalow.

Mac and Gina heard the commotion and came outside, with their friends trailing behind. "What's going on?" Mac asked. "Why are you all back here?"

"Are you sure Samantha has no past medical problems you are aware of?" Officer Sims asked. "How about drug abuse?"

"Oh, well now…let me think for just a minute. You know, I think she may be schizophrenic," Mac said, scratching his ear. "Yeah, that sounds about right. Schizophrenic."

"I don't know about no drug abuse, but she may have mentioned that she's manic-depressive," Gina added.

I shook my head in disbelief. That information would have been helpful when we first arrived! We carefully escorted Samantha back to the ambulance. We had learned our lesson. This time, we made sure she remained seat-belted the entire trip to the hospital.

Mental illness is a serious concern in our country, and a great number of people suffer from it at some point in their lives. I was sincerely glad that Samantha was going to receive help for her condition.

14

Secret Service in Action

*In you, Lᴏʀᴅ my God,
I put my trust.*

PSALM 25:1

> **DISPATCHER:** "Request for fire department and first aid squad at 211 Chestnut Street for a smoke condition in the basement."

"Here we go again," Jessie said, climbing back into the driver's seat, which he had just vacated. "In service," he radioed to the dispatcher.

It had been a busy day. We'd started early in the morning with a first aid call for an elderly woman who complained of feeling weak and nauseated. A few hours later, our squad rushed to help an older gentleman who required rapid takedown after being trapped in his car when it collided with a pickup truck. After that, we'd taken a middle-aged man complaining of fever and chills to the emergency room. Then we responded to another motor vehicle accident, but fortunately, this time no one was injured. We had just returned to our building when the fire call was dispatched.

> **DISPATCHER:** "Update: Officer on the scene reports family burned food in a toaster in a basement kitchenette. Fire is currently out. Proceed with caution."

I watched as members of the fire department used several large fans to remove the smoke from the house. The hot August day had turned into a warm, pleasant night. Lightning bugs danced merrily across the home's front lawn as if in an effort to help light up the scene. I jumped when my pager suddenly went off. *Again.*

DISPATCHER: "Request for first aid for a car in Jensen's Pond with possible entrapment."

"You go on back to the building with Dillon and get another rig for that one. I'll stay here until they wrap things up completely," Jessie said.

"Okay, we'll meet you at the pond when you're done," I replied as we jumped into Dillon's car and returned to the first aid building to get our rescue truck. *Entrapment! That sounds terrible. I hope that by now whoever is stuck inside that car has figured out a way to get out to safety.*

Dillon and I met up with Gary and Colleen at the first aid building. We jumped into the ambulance and headed over to Jensen's Pond. The tall, lush grasses that bordered the pond created popular nesting sites for a variety of ducks and geese. "Car-in-the-lake calls never fail to be interesting," Dillon said.

"You've got that right," Colleen agreed as she parked near the curb by Jensen's Pond. "They don't happen often, but when they do, they're always memorable."

Several streetlamps helped to illuminate the scene. As I peered toward the water, I could see a large, dark-colored sedan with DC plates slowly sinking in the pond. The front end was mostly submerged, but the rear end was still partially out of the water. Small waves lapped gently against the part of the car that was visible. I surmised that the unfortunate driver must not have realized that there was water, rather than a road, directly ahead. Instead of turning left or right, he or she must have plunged straight through the tall ornamental grasses and into the pond.

Despite the late hour, a crowd began gathering at the water's edge. "I'm pretty sure I saw the driver get out and run that way," an older man with a Dalmatian said, pointing down the road. "It's rather dark out tonight, and I was half a block away at the time, but it looked like it may have been a young fellow."

"We'll have to go in the water to check whether there's anyone in the car," Gary said. He quickly stripped off his shirt and shoes, tossing them on the embankment. He waded into the murky water and carefully pulled open the passenger-side door. "I don't see anyone, but I'm going to make sure." With that, he ducked his head under the top edge of the door frame and eased himself into the front section of the car.

I felt for Gary. I mean, I *really* felt for him. If his face touched the water, there was a decent chance he could be swallowing some goose or swan poop within the next few minutes. *Yuck.* I watched as he carefully checked the entire car for any possible victims. After several long moments, Gary reemerged from the car. "There's no one in here," he called out.

"Do me a favor," Officer Endicott directed. "Grab whatever paperwork you can find out of the glove compartment."

Gary worked his way back to the front passenger side of the car, retrieved some wet paperwork, and waded back to shore. As he handed it to Officer Endicott, I maneuvered closer to try to get a peek.

"Secret Service," I heard Officer Endicott whisper to his partner. "We better call the chief to come down here."

Naturally, my ears perked up at the words "Secret Service." I'd found this call interesting to begin with, but it suddenly became a lot more interesting. I had heard a rumor that the Secret Service was in town on a work detail protecting some sort of VIP who was vacationing in Pine Cove. From what I'd heard, they were renting a house just a block away from the site where the car landed in the pond.

Gary climbed out of the water, and I handed him two of our little white first aid towels to dry off. "The car belongs to the Secret Service," I whispered.

At first, Gary looked surprised, but then his face erupted into a smile. "I can't wait to hear the explanation."

A dive team arrived in short order to make an official search. Although Gary had checked inside the car, the dive team searched the area surrounding the car as well. With their wetsuits and scuba gear, they could perform a more comprehensive investigation. "We didn't find anyone," the leader of the dive team said to Officer Endicott when they were finished. I was extremely glad no one had drowned. *It appears the bystander was correct. The driver must have gotten out of the car and left.* So far, it appeared there were no passengers.

"I wouldn't want to be the agent who was driving that car," Dillon said, shaking his head emphatically.

"Yeah, he's probably going to be in a boatload of trouble," I agreed, swatting at a persistent mosquito hovering near my face.

Gary elbowed me in the ribs. "Would you get a load of that?" Like something straight out of a movie, a black sedan with DC plates pulled up. Several men wearing dark suits emerged from the car. They flashed their badges to Officer Endicott. "Secret Service," I heard one of the gentlemen say.

I strained to eavesdrop but could catch only snatches of the conversation.

"The agent left the keys in the ignition."

"We'd like to declare the car stolen."

"We need to do this by the book."

Apparently, one of the agents had just returned to the rental house and had left the car in the driveway with the keys still in the ignition. Allegedly, the car was stolen, but the thief didn't get very far before crashing into Jensen's Pond. Just as my fellow squad members had predicted, the first aid call turned out to be quite memorable. It's the closest I've ever come to seeing our Secret Service in action.

15

The Assault Victim

Do not be far from me,
for trouble is near
and there is no one to help.

PSALM 22:11

Wes Lyons sang loudly along with the car radio as he drove along Hanover Road, occasionally humming when he didn't remember the words. After working a long day as a telecommunications supervisor in the city, he'd grabbed a quick bite to eat on the road. Now he was on his way home and looking forward to relaxing by watching television and eating some microwave popcorn.

When a mischievous raccoon suddenly darted into the road, Wes startled and slammed on his car's brakes. Sensing movement off to the left, he paused and stared out the window into the darkness. *What a dark stretch of road. Looks like a street lamp must be out. But what's that on the ground? That's no raccoon! I really just want to go home, but I guess I should go take a closer look.* Grunting, Wes threw his car into park and swung himself onto the pavement. Realizing how dark it was, he leaned back into the car, reached into the glove compartment, and grabbed a flashlight. *Much better. At least now I'll be able to see a little bit.*

Pausing next to his car, Wes shined the flashlight across the street. *What in the world is that?* He thought that he could just about make out the dim outline of a bicycle lying in the road, close to the gutter. *Uh-oh. Where there's a bike, there may be a rider.*

Swallowing a wave of apprehension, Wes began crossing the street. As he drew closer to the bike, he began to hear soft moaning sounds. Fighting a sense of unease, he flashed the light onto the grass close to the curb. *I sure wish this flashlight was brighter. It's hard to make out anything. It sounds like a person moaning, but I hope it's just a cat or some other animal.* The moaning grew louder, and suddenly his flashlight's beam illuminated a young girl with long dark hair, lying facedown in the grass. He cringed when he noticed that her pants were down around her ankles. He knelt next to the girl and gently tapped her shoulder. "Miss, are you okay?" he asked.

The girl didn't respond to Wes's question and continued to moan. Unsure of what to do, he rolled her to her side and shined the light on her face. He noticed blood oozing from her lip. *I need to get some help.* Just then, he saw headlights in the distance. Jumping to his feet, he stepped to the road and flagged down a passing motorist.

A middle-aged woman in a small sedan stopped and lowered her window. "Can I help you?" she asked. "Wes, is that you?"

"Oh, Keesha, I'm so glad it's you! Yes, it's me, Wes Lyons." He pointed to the side of the road. "Can you please call for help? I found this girl on the side of the road. I'm not sure if she was hit by a car or what. I don't have my cell phone with me, and I don't want to leave her here alone while I try to get help."

"Of course," Keesha replied. "I live only two blocks from here. I'll call the police as soon as I get home." With that, she put her car in gear and sped away.

Wes returned to the young girl's side. This time, she stirred and opened her eyes. "Is he gone?" she cried, her eyes darting to the left and then the right.

"Is who gone?" Wes asked with concern.

"The man," she replied, briefly closing her eyes as if to shut out a bad memory.

"What man?" Wes asked, a prickle of apprehension causing the hairs on his neck to stand up. He shined the light in each direction, looking for signs that someone else might be close by.

"There was a man. He threw me off my bike, and he pulled down my pants, and he…" The young teen burst into tears and didn't finish the sentence. She didn't have to. Her implication was clear.

"The police are on the way, miss. They'll be able to help you," Wes said. "Can you tell me your name?"

"Debbie," she whispered. "I want my mom."

> **DISPATCHER:** "Request for first aid in the road near Pine Cove Park on Hanover Road for an unknown medical emergency."

As Alec, Meg, and I approached Hanover Road, our pagers beeped again with an update.

> **DISPATCHER:** "As per patrols on scene, expedite to Hanover Road for an assault victim."

Alec flipped on the ambulance's flood lights to illuminate the first aid scene. As Meg and I walked briskly toward our victim, yellow and brown leaves crunched under my feet and others tumbled merrily down the road in the cool autumn breeze. I found our patient lying on her left side, close to the edge of the road. I frowned when I noticed her pants were down by her ankles. For some reason, when the dispatcher said assault victim, I assumed that someone had been kicked or punched. Now I realized that this appeared to be a very different type of assault. *An evil, malicious kind. This type of thing doesn't happen in our town. This type of thing isn't supposed to happen anywhere.*

Meg and I knelt next to the young girl. "What's your name, sweetie?" Meg asked.

"Debbie Ward," she whispered, fear shining in her eyes. "Is my mom here yet?"

"Your mother should be here any minute. Can you tell us what happened?" I asked gently.

Tears slid down Debbie's cheeks, and I silently handed her a tissue. "I was riding my bike home with my friends," she said. "Somehow, I got behind them, and I couldn't see them anymore. Then a man came out of the shadows. He pulled me off my bike and pulled down my pants, and then he…"

Debbie began sobbing, and Meg gently patted her shoulder. "It's going to be okay," she said reassuringly. "Your mom will be here any minute. We're going to take you to the hospital to get checked out. The doctors will probably run some tests on you."

Debbie's eyes opened wide. "They can run tests on me? Will it hurt?"

"No, it won't hurt," Meg said. "The hospital staff will be very gentle." She smoothed some of Debbie's stray hairs away from her face.

"Did you get hurt when he pulled you off the bike?" I asked, trying to determine if we needed to use a collar and backboard.

"No, I landed on the grass," she replied. "Nothing hurts. I'm just really scared."

"You don't need to be afraid anymore. We're right here with you. Meg and I are going to help you stand up and take you into the ambulance," I said.

Debbie nodded her head in agreement. We each put an arm under her shoulders and pulled her to her feet. We helped her pull her pants back up. Slowly, the three of us made our way a few feet over to the stretcher. After Debbie lay down on it, we rolled it over to the ambulance and lifted it inside.

Just after we clicked the stretcher into place, Debbie's mother, Mrs. Ward, arrived at the scene. She jumped into the back of the ambulance and threw herself on top of her daughter. "Oh, my poor baby. Are you okay? Who did this to you? Did you see him? I'm here now, honey. Everything's going to be okay. Daddy will meet us at the hospital."

"Oh, Mom, it was terrible!" Debbie collapsed into another fit of gut-wrenching sobs. *This is so awful. This poor, defenseless girl. I feel so sorry for her. What a terrible violation of a young girl's innocence.*

"If you like, you can ride to the hospital back here with us. You just need to put on your seat belt," I said. I figured she would want to stay close to her daughter.

She nodded and buckled her seatbelt. "Thank you for helping Debbie," she said. "I think I'm in shock. I can't stop crying. I feel like I just stepped into a horrible nightmare." She pulled a tissue from her pocket and began dabbing at the tears that trickled down her cheeks.

"I'm so sorry you all have to go through this," I said, though I felt my words were inadequate. I realized this was truly a family in crisis.

"The paramedics aren't available, so we're ready to take off for the hospital," Meg called up to Alec, who was sitting in the driver's seat. "A nice, easy ride." Meg and I tried to make Debbie as comfortable as possible with blankets and pillows. With sadness, I realized that it would take time and love to make her feel better on the inside.

"I just don't understand," Mrs. Ward said. "Where did your friends go? Didn't they notice you were missing? Why in the world would they leave you all by yourself?"

The question hung unanswered in the air. Debbie closed her eyes and started to cry again. Her hands gripped the stretcher's side rails so tightly that her knuckles started turning white.

"Honey, please don't cry. Just wait until I get a hold of your friends' mothers. Can you imagine? Leaving you all alone! And just look what happened!" Mrs. Ward exclaimed.

The back of the ambulance fell into silence, each of us deep in our own thoughts. I was glad when we arrived at the emergency room a few moments later. I knew Debbie would receive excellent care here, not just for her physical wounds but also psychological counseling. We had called ahead, so I knew they'd have a crisis counselor standing by.

Maggie, the triage nurse, met us in the hallway. "I'm going to take you to a private room," she said soothingly. We followed her down the hallway into a small room on the left. As Meg explained the situation to Maggie, Alec and I carefully transferred Debbie from our stretcher to the hospital's.

Maggie came close to Debbie's face. I watched as Maggie inhaled deeply, and then her brow furrowed. "Debbie, is there anything else you want to tell me about what happened tonight?" she asked.

"What do you mean?" Debbie stammered, a few beads of sweat starting to break out on her forehead.

"Did you drink alcohol tonight?" Maggie asked.

"Excuse me, nurse, but Debbie's only 14. She doesn't drink," Mrs. Ward said, a puzzled look flashing across her face.

"Is your daughter a diabetic?"

"No."

"I smell a fruity odor on Debbie's breath. Sometimes that can be the result of diabetes. Other times, it can be caused by drinking. If you did have something to drink tonight, I want you to know you're not in trouble. It's just important for us to know so we can give you the best possible care."

"I had a few beers," Debbie admitted in a small voice.

"Okay. Well, since you were assaulted, I'm going to have the doctor come in now and give you a special exam."

Debbie looked decidedly uncomfortable. "About that. There wasn't really a man. I stopped and got off my bike because I had to pee."

"And then you fell and had trouble standing back up?" Maggie guessed.

"Yes," Debbie said, her shoulders slumping.

"Did your friends get scared that you were going to get them in trouble, so they left you?"

"Yes." Debbie sighed miserably. "I made the whole thing up so my parents wouldn't find out we were drinking."

"Debbie," Mrs. Ward said, "I simply cannot believe this. Are you sure? Is what you're saying true?"

Tears began trickling down Debbie's cheeks. "I'm sorry, Mom."

I was flabbergasted. I had fallen for Debbie's story, hook, line, and sinker. Usually I can smell alcohol on people's breath, but I hadn't detected it on Debbie's. Of course, I hadn't been looking for it either. I peeked at Alec and Meg. They both looked equally surprised.

Sensing the sudden tension in the room, I grabbed a corner of our empty stretcher and backed slowly out of the room. Meg caught hold of the other end and followed behind me. It looked to me like this family needed some time to iron this out privately.

Although it was unfortunate that Debbie had gone on an underage drinking binge, it was much better than the alternative. I was relieved that there was not a malicious attacker on the loose after all.

16

Left Behind

*Our mouths were filled with laughter, our tongues
with songs of joy. Then it was said among the
nations, "The LORD has done great things for them."*

PSALM 126:2

Olivia Kendall had been in a rush for as long as she could remember. Now that she was almost 80, she was still rushing. She had only one speed, and it seemed to be permanently set to "fast." It wasn't that she was intentionally quick on her feet. It was just that she had long legs and with them came long strides. It was a real effort to walk slowly.

I could use a cup of nice hot coffee. I'll start the coffee maker now, and then Tammy and I can each have some. Olivia had been living with her daughter, Tammy, ever since Tammy's husband had died about three years before from throat cancer. Olivia's husband had passed away ten years ago, so it seemed only natural for mother and daughter to live together.

Olivia popped out of bed, donned a pair of slippers, and sped down the hallway and through the living room. As she rounded the corner into the kitchen, her right foot hit a small wet spot on the floor. Since Olivia was moving so fast, she didn't have a chance to regain her balance. Before she could fully process what was happening, she landed with a loud thud flat on her back. Almost in disbelief, she stared up at the wooden beams in her pine ceiling. *If I hurt myself, I'm going to have an absolute fit!* Carefully, she tried to turn her neck from side to side. *So far, so good.* Next, she opened and closed her hands, and then she bent and straightened her elbows. *Nothing broken there.* She cautiously wiggled her feet and then bent each hip and knee. *Thank you, Lord, I think I'm okay.*

"Mom...Mom, is that you? Are you okay? Did you fall?" Tammy asked anxiously. "Where are you?" she called from upstairs.

"Down here, dusting the kitchen floor," Olivia grumbled. "With my bottom."

Tammy rushed downstairs and knelt beside her mother. "Don't move. I'm going to call for an ambulance."

"Don't you dare! I'm fine! There is absolutely no reason to call those people. Nothing's hurt. I just need a little help to get up," Olivia said, a deep frown connecting some of the wrinkles on her forehead.

"Mom, I really think it's better if they come and at least check you out. If you're okay, then you can stay home," she reasoned.

"That's what worries me. What if they say I'm not okay when I know perfectly well that I am? What if they don't want to take no for an answer and try to make me go to the hospital?" Olivia asked grouchily.

"Now, Mom, I don't think they're going to make you go to the emergency room if you're fine. Let's have them check your blood pressure and stuff," Tammy said.

"What if we can't get them to leave?" Olivia asked, obviously not convinced.

"Well, I really don't think the volunteers are going to stay here all day if you decide not to go to the hospital," Tammy replied, hiding a smile. Her mother was sometimes prone to being a bit on the theatrical side. "They'll just want to make sure that you're okay, and I want to make sure you can walk."

Olivia sighed loudly. "Does it matter if I say no? If I say don't call them?"

"No, I'm calling them right now. For peace of mind. Sorry, Mom." Tammy stood and reached for the phone.

"Sorry my foot," Olivia muttered. "All I know is that I am *not* going to the hospital!"

....

DISPATCHER: "Request for first aid at 2048 Wesley Avenue for an
elderly fall victim."

Helen, Archie, Colleen, Jillian DeMarco, and I piled into the
ambulance.

"I'm barely awake," Jillian said. "I went on two first aid calls last
night, and then my dog woke me up really early." Jillian spent morn-
ings volunteering at the local library and spent much of her free time
answering first aid calls.

"Then you're the perfect person to fill out our call sheet," Helen said,
handing her the clipboard with a smile. "It'll keep you awake."

"Gee, thanks," she grumbled good-naturedly. "Why don't you all
relax in the rig and I'll take care of everything?"

Archie parked the ambulance in front of a gray colonial with a
pretty fieldstone exterior, taking care not to scratch the rig's roof on
the century-old sycamore branches that draped across the street. Jillian, call sheet in hand, headed toward the front porch while the rest of
us followed close behind with our first aid equipment.

A middle-aged woman with short brown hair met us at the door.
"Hi. Thanks so much for coming," she whispered, glancing furtively
behind her. "I just wanted to warn you that my mother isn't thrilled
that I called you."

"I can hear you whispering!" a female voice bellowed from the
kitchen. "I'm not deaf, and I'm not going to the hospital!"

Sounds like this might be a quick refusal. If a patient is of sound mind
and is adamant about not going to the hospital after we do our assessment, we simply have the person sign a release form.

We stepped into the kitchen and found an older woman lying on
her back, with a pillow tucked underneath her head. "Slipped on a wet
spot," she grumbled. "Can't imagine why it was there. Kindly just get
me up, and then you can all be on your way." She wriggled uncomfortably on the ground. "Thank you," she added, almost as an afterthought.

Jillian stepped off to the side with Tammy and asked her a bunch of questions for our run sheet. Helen checked Olivia's vital signs. "Everything's normal," she said. "How about we try getting you up on your feet?"

"I've been ready to get up on my feet for ten minutes. This floor is not very comfortable," Olivia replied. I knew she wasn't truly upset with us. She was berating herself for falling.

Archie and I eased Olivia onto her feet and led her to a nearby kitchen chair. "How do you feel?" I asked.

"Much better now," she said. "Mainly just embarrassed to bring you all out here. And mad at myself for losing my balance like that."

"Accidents happen to all of us," Archie said. "Don't be so hard on yourself. The main thing is that you're okay."

"Just call us back if you need us or if something starts to hurt," I added.

We gathered our equipment and headed back without delay to our first aid building. My stomach grumbled, and I envisioned a nice bowl of cereal with a banana for breakfast.

"I'm going to check if this oxygen tank is full," Helen said. "Andrea, do you mind marking up the call board?"

"I'm on it," I replied. The call board allows us to keep track of which members are present for calls. After marking the board, I asked, "Where's the call sheet?"

"I'll check the ambulance," Archie said, climbing into the rear of the rig.

"I'll check the front, by the driver's seat," Colleen offered.

"No luck," Archie said, frowning. "Where could it be?"

"That's funny. It's not up front either," Colleen added.

"The last person to have the call sheet was Jillian," Helen said, tightening the valve on the oxygen tank.

We all looked at each other and then exclaimed in unison, "Jillian!" *No Jillian.* As in, we had left Jillian standing in Olivia Kendall's kitchen. We had driven away without her!

Helen and I unsuccessfully fought the urge to giggle. I recalled a first aid call several years earlier in which we had accidentally forgotten one of our members in the emergency room. On our way home from the hospital, the police dispatcher called our ambulance to let us know we had left a member behind. This time we had forgotten a member in a patient's house! "Jillian's not going to be happy with us," Helen said, stifling a laugh.

"Yes, I wouldn't be too happy with you guys if you forgot me at the scene," Archie agreed as he climbed back into the driver's seat and the rest of us piled into the ambulance.

Just then, a small blue sedan pulled onto the apron of the first aid building, and a red-faced Jillian climbed out of the front passenger seat. I could hear her turn to the driver and say, "Thank you for the ride." I strained to get a better look. Sure enough, it was Tammy Kendall behind the wheel. Lowering the window, she waved and called out, "Thanks again for your help!"

To her credit, Jillian waited until Tammy pulled away before asking in an accusing voice, "How long did it take you to notice I was missing?"

We all apologized profusely before erupting into fits of laughter. Perhaps it's because we witness so much sadness, or maybe I'm just making excuses, but sometimes we enjoy a good laugh. Because she is so good-natured, Jillian took the whole thing in stride. Sometimes, I think a good laugh is the best medicine for health care providers!

17

The Good Samaritan and the Foot Chase

*He answered, "'Love the Lord your God with all your heart
and with all your soul and with all your strength and with
all your mind'; and, 'Love your neighbor as yourself.'"*

LUKE 10:27

The sound of the first aid pager beeping loudly startled me out of a deep sleep. Although I'm usually a light sleeper, I always set my pager to full volume at night to ensure that I wake up. I'm not sure of the exact decibel level, but suffice it to say that it's LOUD.

> **DISPATCHER:** "Request for first aid at 609 Hudson Avenue for a 15-year-old intoxicated male."

I threw on some clothes and slid my feet into my sneakers. Before I could get out the door, my pager went off again.

> **DISPATCHER:** "You have a second call. Request for first aid at 220 Crestview Drive for an 88-year-old male with an altered mental status."

When I parked at our first aid building, both ambulances were already pulling onto the concrete apron. "Hop into this one," Helen called to me through the driver's side window of one of the rigs. Kevin Wong was in the passenger seat next to her, buckling his seatbelt. Kevin had recently graduated from college and was considering going to graduate school to become a psychologist.

"Which call are we going to?" I asked, automatically grabbing a pair of medium nylon gloves from the dispenser before taking a seat.

"We have a crew to cover the second call," Helen explained. "We're going to the first one. Jessie's going to meet us at the scene."

Helen flipped on the emergency lights and shifted into gear. "We're responding to 609 Hudson Avenue," she advised dispatch. As we turned left out of our first aid driveway and headed west, I watched through our rear window as the other ambulance headed east. It was a warm night, so I flipped on the air conditioner switch before grabbing our patient clipboard and an emesis basin (in case our patient vomited).

"Be advised, the patient is in and out of consciousness," Dispatcher Franklin said. "You have one member on the scene."

A few moments later, Helen pulled in front of a white Victorian with royal blue trim. As I stepped out the side door of the ambulance, I noticed a dark blue SUV was parked in the driveway with the rear doors open. Kevin grabbed the first aid jump kit from the side compartment, and we hustled toward the vehicle. As we got closer, I could see that Jessie was bent over, his head inside the rear of the vehicle. When he realized we were behind him, he stood back up. "This is Caden Mayer. His mother just picked him up from a house party. As they got closer to home, he started vomiting and then passed out. She pulled into the driveway and called 911."

Silently, I handed Jessie a blood pressure cuff, stethoscope, and emesis basin. I began jotting down what Jessie had described in the summary section of the call sheet. Kevin slipped into the rear of the SUV from the other side so he could support Caden's head and protect his airway. I headed toward Caden's mother, who was standing with Sergeant Flint. He was breaking the news to her that her son was intoxicated. She seemed absolutely astounded by the possibility. "You must be mistaken," she said. "I think he's coming down with something. Or he has food poisoning."

"Excuse me…may I ask you a few questions?" I began. After she nodded, I questioned her about Caden's date of birth, medical history, and whether he was taking any medications or allergic to any.

"I just can't believe it," she said after answering my questions. "Caden is such a good boy. He would never drink. Maybe someone slipped something into his soda."

"Well, they can certainly check into that at the hospital," I said, trying to ease some of her anxiety. I knew from previous first aid calls that the odds were that Caden and his friends had somehow gotten access to alcohol and decided to give it a try. Caden would most likely be having a heart-to-heart conversation with his parents when this was all over. But for now, we needed to focus on getting him safely to the emergency room.

"I have to get some stuff from the house," Mrs. Mayer said. "Is it okay if I meet you at the hospital?"

"Yes, of course," I replied. "But I don't think that they can do much until you get there. They need a parent or guardian present." Mrs. Mayer nodded and crossed over the driveway to her son. His eyes were closed, but he opened them halfway when his mother tapped his shoulder to say goodbye. He grunted an unintelligible reply and closed his eyes once more.

Kevin and Jessie carefully pivoted Caden from the SUV onto the stretcher, and then Helen and Jessie steered it across the brick pavers to the ambulance. "Kevin, why don't you stay in town in case we have another call?" Jessie suggested. "You can drive my car back to the first aid building, and I'll go to the hospital with Helen and Andrea."

"Sounds like a plan," Kevin replied. "Are the medics available yet?"

"No, not yet," Sergeant Flint said. "Should I cancel them?"

"Yes, that's fine," Jessie said, passing his car keys to Kevin. "We're going to get moving."

Caden began crying and moaning once we loaded him into the ambulance, but the rhythmic swaying of the rig quickly lulled him back to sleep. I put a blood pressure cuff back on his arm to reassess his vital signs: "Blood pressure is still up a bit, 130 over 90. His heart rate is 92 and regular, and his respiratory rate is 14." Jessie handed me a penlight to check his pupils. "They're equal and reactive to light."

The rest of the trip to Bakersville Hospital passed uneventfully. Soon I was giving the patient report to Maggie, the triage nurse. "Where's his mother or father?" she asked.

"His mother is on the way. She should be here any minute," I replied, straightening the pillow behind Caden's head.

"Well, if you don't mind, please stay with him until she gets here," Maggie said. "We can't do much until we get his mother's consent."

"No problem," I replied, glancing at my watch. The minutes ticked by slowly. Our other ambulance arrived with their patient, an elderly gentleman who had become confused and disoriented during the night. Jessie and Helen helped our other crew transfer him from our stretcher to the hospital's gurney.

"I guess we'll see you back at the building," Jessie said. "We're kind of hung up here."

I glanced yet again at my watch. *Where in the world is his mother?*

"Are you sure she's on her way?" Maggie asked, as if reading my thoughts.

"She said she'd be right behind us," I replied. "I'm not really sure where she could be." Caden turned to his left side, continuing to sleep off the effects of too much booze.

"Well, I guess you can go," Maggie said. "We'll take it from here, thanks."

She didn't have to tell me twice. It was now past midnight, and I had to get up early for work. I hurried down the long corridor and climbed into the back of the ambulance. Helen and Jessie were already in their seats, ready to go.

"So, his mother finally came?" Helen asked, smoothly pulling the ambulance out of its parking spot.

"No, but thank goodness Maggie decided I could go." I settled into the captain's chair, which is the front-most seat in the back of the ambulance.

About halfway between the hospital and home, Helen eased into the left turn lane. "Uh-oh," she said. "It looks like we might have some sort of trouble ahead. There's a guy standing in the median, flagging us down."

I craned my head toward the front of the rig and peered to the left. Sure enough, there was a man who looked to be about 40 years old, frantically waving his arms at us. "You better put on our lights so we don't get rear-ended," I said, grabbing a pair of gloves. One thing I've learned from working in a trauma center is that sometimes it's the ones who stop to help that end up being injured. The emergency lights would give us at least some protection.

Helen lowered her window, and the man rushed up to our rig. "Help! There's an unconscious man in that car," he said excitedly, pointing to a black SUV stopped in front of our ambulance.

"Do you think he might have had a heart attack?" Helen wondered aloud.

"Let's check it out," Jessie said, hopping out of the rig.

"Be careful," Helen said. She picked up the mic and called directly to the dispatcher of the town we were driving through, Marina Beach. "We've been flagged down by a motorist in front of the Marina Beach Deli for an unconscious male in a car. Please send a patrol car to assist us," she said calmly.

Jessie and I joined the Good Samaritan on the median. "I pulled up behind him," he explained. "The light turned green, but he didn't budge. I honked, and he still didn't move. I started to pull around his car, but when I looked inside, he was slumped over the steering wheel and looked unconscious. I thought he might be dead or something. I parked my car in front of his and tapped on his window. He didn't respond at all. I looked up and saw you coming, so that's when I started waving to get your attention."

"Okay, we'll see what's going on," Jessie said. We peered into the car, and sure enough, there was a man slumped over the steering wheel. Jessie pulled the driver's side door open with his left hand and stepped up, placing his right foot on the running board.

It was quite dark, and a nearby streetlamp didn't provide much light. *Is the man okay? Did he have a heart attack? Is he dead?* I didn't have much time to wonder because the SUV suddenly began moving forward. "Jessie, grab on!" I shouted.

"I'm trying!" he yelled, grabbing the upper frame with his right hand

and the door with his left. His right leg was inside the car, but his left leg was sailing in the open air. "I need to reach the brakes!" he shouted.

The SUV continued rolling forward along the road. "I've got to move my car!" the Good Samaritan shouted, desperately rushing toward his vehicle. I glanced toward his car in the distance and quickly did the math. Barring a miracle, there was no way he would be able to reach his car in time.

I raced alongside next to Jessie, hoping I could somehow catch him and break his fall should he let go. As I ran, I glanced back at our rig, which was now at least 40 feet behind us. I knew that Helen would try to get us help, and I fervently hoped that it would come in time!

"Marina Bay PD from the Pine Cove First Aid, he's trying to make a getaway! We're doing the best we can!" Helen exclaimed.

What unfolded next took only seconds, but it seemed to last an eternity. The SUV continued to rush along with Jessie clinging on for dear life as I sprinted next to him. I dodged a street sign and then jumped off the curb and into the road as I tried to stay as close as possible to him.

We're getting closer and closer to the Good Samaritan's car. He's never going to be able to move it in time! He was just now reaching his car, but we were quickly bearing down on it.

The SUV smashed against the rear of the Good Samaritan's car, and it surged forward several feet from the impact. I cringed as I saw Jessie's head bounce off the upper door frame of the SUV. He let go and staggered backward, so I grabbed him from behind by his shoulders. "I'm okay," he said, wiping blood off his forehead. "Go check on him," he added, pointing to our formerly unconscious patient. It appeared as though he had woken up from the impact and all the excitement.

"Is the car off?" I asked. There was no way I wanted to end up in the same boat as Jessie, with the car somehow taking off with me hanging on!

"Yeah, I got it. You can go in from the passenger side."

Watching for traffic, I slipped around the front of the SUV and climbed into the passenger seat. "Sir, are you okay?" I asked. A strong odor of alcohol greeted me. *He's as drunk as a skunk.*

He looked at me, his eyes wide and frightened. "No speak English," he murmured, shrugging his shoulders. From a glance, he didn't appear to be injured.

Before I could say anything else, Marina Bay police cars began arriving from every direction, lights flashing and sirens wailing. I was impressed that they'd come so quickly to help us.

Jessie, continuing to ignore his own injury, climbed into the rear of the SUV to stabilize the patient's cervical spine until we could better determine whether he was hurt. *Just like Jessie. Even when injured himself, he puts the needs of others in front of his own.*

As I checked our patient from head to toe, I could hear the police interviewing the Good Samaritan. Fortunately, the SUV hit his trailer hitch, so the car itself was basically undamaged.

Our patient was uninjured, so I knew the next stop for him would be a sobriety test and a trip to the Marina Bay Police Department. Jessie and I shook hands with the Good Samaritan before departing. "You know what they say—no good deed goes unpunished," he said, smiling ruefully.

I reflected that it was all a matter of timing. If Caden's mother hadn't been so delayed getting to the emergency room, we would have passed by the scene of the incident long before it unfolded. We surmised that when Jessie opened the SUV's door, the man woke up just enough for his foot to slip off the brake or to press down on the accelerator.

Driving under the influence snatches countless innocent lives each year. It was a blessing that our patient was found and stopped before he accidentally injured or even killed someone. It was a miracle that Jessie wasn't more seriously injured. *Thank you, God, for keeping us safe tonight!*

18

Touched by an Angel-Child

*They can no longer die; for they are like the angels. They are
God's children, since they are children of the resurrection.*

LUKE 20:36

Allie Hartman opened her eyes and looked up at the ceiling fan. It
spun around and around, much as it did every night. The repetitive motion brought her comfort. Allie peered through the white slats
of her bedrail. The house was dark and quiet, and she was glad her
night-light was on. She liked the way it glowed and lit up her collection
of princess figurines on her bookshelf. Sometimes, the nights seemed
long and lonely, and she missed seeing her mom and dad. Allie liked
the daytime much better.

She rubbed her chest and coughed. She knew that whenever she
coughed, her mother would rush in and suction the hole in her throat that
she breathed though. She hated coughing, but she loved seeing her mom.

I don't feel so good. I hope Mom comes in soon. Allie felt as if an electrical storm was brewing inside her head. She knew the feeling well
because it had happened a few times before.

....

DISPATCHER: "Request for first aid at 416 Bergen Street for a child
having a seizure."

Jose Sanchez, who had recently retired from a career in politics, arrived at the first aid building at the same time Helen and I did. "I'll drive," he said, so Helen and I jumped in the back of the ambulance and started prepping equipment for the call.

"The address doesn't sound familiar to me," Helen said, reaching for the pediatric kit.

"Me neither." I filled in the address at the top of the call sheet. "I don't think I've been there before."

A couple of minutes later, we pulled up in front of a gray clapboard house on a quiet residential street a short distance from our squad building. I was glad to see that a Pine Cove patrol car was already parked out front. A streetlight helped to light the sidewalk in front of the home, and we hurried toward the front porch. Festive red Christmas lights decorated the porch railing and the front door.

I knocked on the door and then pushed it open. "Hello?" I called out as Jose, Helen, and I stepped inside. We followed the sound of voices through the living room and down a narrow hallway to a small bedroom in the rear of the home.

A woman in her mid-thirties stood next to a large hospital-style crib. She was busy suctioning phlegm from a young girl's tracheostomy—a surgical opening in the trachea (windpipe) that allows for easier breathing. I could tell from the ease with which she performed the task that she had done it many times. A well-loved brown teddy bear, which was missing one eye, sat on the foot of the bed.

The child's small body was consumed by tonic-clonic (formerly called grand mal) seizures, causing her arms and legs to shake violently. Her mother, a kind-looking woman with warm brown eyes, looked up as we entered the room. "Hi, I'm Vicky Hartman, and this is my daughter, Allie. I woke up because I heard her coughing. When I came into the room, I could see that she was having a seizure." Mrs. Hartman glanced at her watch. "She's probably been seizing for six or seven minutes."

A tall man with short dark hair, who looked to be about 40, entered the room and gently squeezed Mrs. Hartman's shoulder. Then he quickly stepped toward the back corner of the room, as if trying to stay out of the way. He looked decidedly pale and leaned against the wall for support. *He must be the little girl's father. This must be so frightening for him to witness.*

Sergeant Flint passed me a small slip of paper with Allie's name and date of birth for our call sheet. "Mrs. Hartman can fill you in on Allie's medical history," he said.

I marveled at how Mrs. Hartman was somehow managing to stay calm despite the dire situation. Her composure stood in sharp contrast to the state in which we usually find the unfortunate parents of children with medical emergencies. *I wonder if she's a nurse.*

"Allie's got quite a complicated medical history," Mrs. Hartman explained. "I know she doesn't look it, but she's actually seven years old. She was born about three months early and has some medical problems, including cerebral palsy. She's had seizures before, but never for this long."

I noticed that there was a bluish hue around Allie's lips. "I don't think she's getting enough air," I said. Quickly, I counted her respiratory rate. "Her respiratory rate is too low. We need to assist her breathing." I hooked up our child-sized bag valve mask directly to her tracheostomy and began assisting her ventilations. My hands grew sweaty, causing my gloves to cling to my fingers and palms. I had done rescue breathing dozens of times, but never on such a young child.

The paramedics, Arthur and Kennisha, arrived a moment later. I knew Allie was in good hands. "How long has she been seizing at this point?" Arthur asked.

"About 15 minutes," Helen answered. "We were just about to bring her out to the ambulance."

"Okay, hang on for a bit and we'll just take a moment to establish an IV line before we start rolling," Kennisha said, pulling an intravenous setup from her kit.

"She's always a tough stick," Mrs. Hartman warned. "The phlebotomist often has a very difficult time when we go for bloodwork." She leaned over and, brushing away a strand of Allie's hair, gently kissed her daughter's forehead. From working as a physical therapist, I've observed that being a parent of a child with special needs can be very uplifting but often challenging too. I could only surmise that the road that the Hartmans had traveled had been a difficult one at times.

Kennisha attempted to get an IV line in each of Allie's arms, without success. "Let's get her in the rig," she finally said. "We need to get moving. We can get the IV on the way."

In the ambulance, Arthur tried without luck to get an IV in Allie's left hand. Helen took over squeezing the BVM while I suctioned more phlegm from her tracheostomy. I noticed that Arthur slid farther down the bench and pulled the leg of Allie's pajama bottom up over her knee. Next, he started prepping an area on Allie's lower leg.

"What are you doing?" Helen asked the question I was about to ask myself.

"An interosseous IV," Arthur responded, placing the point of a large needle on Allie's lower leg. "We need to get access, and we need to get it right now."

I had heard of an interosseous IV, but I had never seen one performed in the field. *Arthur and Kennisha are going to put the IV directly into Allie's tibia bone.* I realized that it was very dangerous for Allie to continue seizing for so long. The paramedics needed to provide her lifesaving medications right away.

Arthur and Kennisha placed an interosseous IV into Allie's left tibia. Helen and I cringed, though Allie appeared oblivious to the procedure. I felt a sense of relief when we arrived at the emergency room. Although we were still assisting Allie's breathing, I was grateful that she still had a pulse. A pediatric team met us at the doors and ushered us directly into a treatment room. After all this time, she was still seizing and continued to struggle to breathe. I knew that her young life hung in the balance. It was touch and go at this point. I said a quick silent prayer that she'd pull through this and be okay.

The next day, I ran into Helen on another first aid call. "I heard that Allie got admitted to the pediatric intensive care unit," she said. "She's holding her own."

I breathed a sigh of relief that she was still alive. "That's really good news!" I hoped that she would rally and recover quickly. A few weeks later, I was thrilled to learn that she was discharged home. *Thank you, Lord, for letting Allie spend Christmas at home with her family.*

....

Allie Hartman blinked her eyes and looked up at the ceiling fan. It was spinning around and around, just as it did every night. But something was different tonight. She saw a very bright light, and it seemed to be calling to her. The light was warm and bright; it wasn't scary at all. It seemed to envelope her in a loving embrace. *Maybe I should go toward it.*

> **DISPATCHER:** "Request for first aid at 416 Bergen Street for an unconscious, unresponsive child."

On a Wednesday night, exactly five weeks later, we were called back to Allie's house. I felt apprehensive. Allie had barely clung to life the last time we were there.

Helen recognized the address too. "Sounds like Allie again," she said as we climbed into the ambulance. "I wonder if she's having another seizure."

I frowned, recalling the first time we met Allie. "The dispatcher said unconscious and unresponsive. That sure doesn't sound good."

When Helen and I arrived at Allie's home, an ice-cold biting wind chased us to the front door. This time, I noticed that the street light was out, making it more challenging to see the way. The pretty Christmas lights that had decorated the front porch weeks before had been taken down. I hoped that the darkness wasn't a foreshadowing of what we might find inside.

We found Allie exactly as the dispatcher had described her—completely unresponsive. Her tiny body lay motionless on the bed, making her look as if she were a doll instead of a little girl. Although Mrs. Hartman was sobbing, she still had the presence of mind to grab Allie's BVM from next to her bed and had begun rescue breathing before we arrived. Mr. Hartman, his eyes filled with pain and fear, hovered close by.

Helen reached down and felt along Allie's neck for a carotid pulse. *Please, please let Allie have a pulse.* "No pulse," Helen said. She took over the bag valve mask from Mrs. Hartman. I started chest compressions. I tried to block out the heart-wrenching sobs of Allie's mother and instead focus on Allie and her ventilations and compressions. I glanced at Helen. She appeared to be having a hard time too. Neither of us had ever performed CPR on such a young child.

Allie's eyes were dull and unfocused. Her pupils were already dilating, which was not a good sign. *I'm afraid that we're going to lose her.* Arthur and Kennisha, the same paramedic team that had assisted Allie last month, arrived within a few minutes. *At least they're already familiar with her case.*

"Mrs. Hartman put Allie to bed a little while ago, and she had just come back in to check on her. She realized that Allie wasn't responding, so she called for her husband to dial 911. When she realized that Allie wasn't breathing, she initiated rescue breathing with a BVM," Helen explained to Arthur and Kennisha.

"I just don't understand why this is happening," Mrs. Hartman managed to say, as she stroked her daughter's arm. *The love of a mother for her daughter is a bond like nothing else.*

I began to experience a strange sensation of déjà vu. Arthur and Kennisha tried unsuccessfully to start an IV line in each of Allie's arms. When that failed, they created an interosseous IV line in her left tibia. Arthur began pushing medications through the IV access in earnest. "Okay," Arthur said. "We need to get moving. Let's get her into the ambulance."

As I glanced at the old teddy bear on Allie's bed and the toys on her bookshelf, I felt a profound sadness. *Why does such a young person have to struggle so hard to survive?*

We piled blankets on top of Allie and rushed her outside and into the ambulance. With lights flashing and sirens wailing, we began the short trip to Bakersville Hospital. As we continued compressing Allie's chest and breathing for her, I was filled with hope that she would somehow pull through. That she would "make it." That she would go home and play and smile again. The sound of Mrs. Hartman's crying still rang in my ears. I watched as Helen squeezed the bag valve mask. The seconds seemed to tick by ever so slowly. *Still no pulse.*

Once again, the pediatric response team met us at the emergency room doors and directed us into a treatment room. Feverishly, they made every possible effort to revive little Allie. But this time, it was not to be. Within 15 minutes, Allie was pronounced. Nausea gripped me, and a profound heaviness tugged at my heart. I had never seen a child die before. I couldn't begin to imagine the pain and grief that Allie's family was experiencing. *How will her parents go on without her?* I recognized that Allie's life, although cut tragically short, was nevertheless a precious gift. *I feel like I was just touched by an angel-child.*

....

Many years later, Helen and I stood chatting in front of our squad building after a first aid drill. Suddenly, she grabbed my arm. "Do you recognize who that is?" she asked me, pointing to a woman in a beige car parked close by.

I studied her for a moment, but she didn't seem familiar to me. "No, who?" I asked.

"That's Allie's mother." She didn't have to say another word. It all came rushing back: the hope, the pain, the grief, the loss.

"Do you think she'd mind if we went up and said hello?" I asked.

"No, I think she would be okay with it. Let's do it," Helen said.

We approached her car and gently tapped on the window. Mrs. Hartman lowered the window and smiled. "What can I do for you?" she asked pleasantly.

Helen and I introduced ourselves, explaining that we were at her house all those years ago when Allie passed away.

Allie's mother jumped out of her car and hugged each of us. "Thank you so much for everything you did for us," she said. "You know, we still miss her very much."

Just then, a young teenager approached the car. "This is my son,

Bill," she said. "Unfortunately, he never got to meet Allie in person, but we've told him lots of stories about her."

"I really wish I could have met my sister," he said, tugging wistfully on the rim of his baseball cap.

"You would have loved her," Helen said.

"She was truly special," I added, feeling choked up. After all these years, I can still picture Allie in her bedroom as if it were yesterday, her well-loved teddy bear keeping her steady company. I think of her as an angel, watching over the little brother she never had a chance to meet.

19

Going to the Birds

I trust in your unfailing love;
my heart rejoices in your salvation.
I will sing the LORD's praise,
for he has been good to me.

PSALM 13:5-6

As I stood at the kitchen sink and rinsed out a soup bowl, I glanced out the window toward our neighbors' house. My eyes zeroed in on a small brown clump of twigs on the ground close to an evergreen bush. Turning off the faucet, I looked over at my mother. "It looks like there may be a nest on the ground near the driveway," I said. "I'm going out to take a look. Do you want to come with me?"

"I'm afraid I already saw it," Mom replied, pausing from peeling an onion. Her eyes misted a bit, and I wasn't sure if it was because of the onion or the nest.

"Why didn't you tell me?" I asked, placing the bowl on the drying rack.

"Because I know how much you love birds, and I didn't want to upset you. I already went out and checked. All the babies are dead, and the parents are gone. It's just awful. I'm not even sure how the nest fell or where it fell from," Mom replied. "I think it may have been tucked into the neighbors' second floor window air conditioner." My mom's always been quick to care for birds that have accidentally flown into windows or been hit by cars. I knew that if there was any chance the birds could have been rescued, she would have given it her best shot.

"I'll go back out in a few minutes to bury them," she said.

"Well, I'm going to look anyway," I said, the first aid squad member within me drawn almost magnetically to "the scene of the accident." I hurried out the back door and directly over to the little upside-down nest. The scene before me was not pretty. One tiny baby sparrow was sprawled dead on the ground, close to the nest. Another dead sibling lay close by. They had most likely expired from the trauma of the fall. *I'm so sorry for these tiniest of God's creatures. They're so small, they can't even fly yet! They barely even had a chance in this world. And their poor parents. They must be shocked and confused, unsure of what went wrong.* Even though the birds were obviously dead, I gently poked one with my finger just to make double-sure. *Nothing.* I still wasn't quite ready to give up. I looked more closely at the mangled, upside-down nest. *I wonder...*

I gently flipped the sparrow nest over so that it was right-side up. And there, wedged into the side of the damaged nest, was one more baby bird. *Could it still be alive?* Carefully, I picked up the tiny speck of life and placed it in the palm of my hand. At first glance, the little bird certainly didn't look alive. His eyes were closed, his neck was twisted funny, and he barely had any feathers. I looked more closely. *I don't believe it! The little guy's chest is rising and falling! He's alive!*

There was no way I was leaving the little baby outside to take his chances with nature. I didn't want a cat or some other predator to have him for a snack. If he was going to die, I'd much rather he passed away in peace in the safety of our home. Quickly, I stood and carried him inside. "Mom, come quick! I found one that's still alive."

"I don't believe it. I checked all around and found only two that were already dead. Where did you find him?" she asked.

"He was under the nest," I explained. "How many minutes has it been since you first noticed it?"

Mom glanced at her watch. "It's probably been at least a half hour," she said. "And I'm not sure how long the nest was on the ground before I saw it. I just wish we'd found him sooner."

"Better late than never. I'm going to call the pet store and see if they can refer us to a wildlife rehabilitator," I said. "I'm not sure how to properly care for him. And anyway, I have a first aid meeting tonight and I have to go to work tomorrow."

"Great idea," Mom said. "I'm more used to handling birds that are just temporarily stunned. I've never cared for a baby before. Maybe they can give us some advice."

The pet store owner, an older gentleman who had run the local shop for as long as I could remember, instructed me on how to care for the baby bird and made arrangements for a specialist to take over care the following morning.

"Well, little fellow, if we're going to be spending the evening together, then you need a name. How about Homer?" I asked, opening my hand and peeking at him. In response, he opened his eyes and blinked a few times. "Homer it is, then," I said, gently stroking his back.

The next few hours passed in a blur of feeding Homer with a medicine dropper and setting up a little spot for him to spend the night. Before I knew it, it was time to go to my first aid meeting.

"What are you going to do with Homer?" Mom asked. "Do you want me to take care of him while you're at the meeting?"

"No, it's okay. I'm going to take him with me, I think. I'll bring his food too, just in case." I figured no one would even realize that I had him with me. I would just keep him tucked in my hand, since he seemed to really enjoy it. I supposed it reminded him of his nest. Homer hadn't made so much as a peep yet, so I wasn't worried about anyone noticing him.

I slid into a seat in the back of the meeting room, trying to keep a low profile. Homer remained content, snuggled inside my hand. My plan to keep Homer without anyone being the wiser appeared to be working.

However, the meeting dragged on (as meetings tend to do), and Homer began to grow restless. He started wiggling in my hand, and I tried to discreetly whisper soothing words to him. I glanced around and breathed a sigh of relief when it appeared no one seemed to notice anything unusual about me.

During a quiet moment of the meeting, Homer let out his first chirp. My elation that he must be feeling better was only slightly dampened by the fact that it was harder to cover up his chirping than it was to disguise his wiggling. I faked a cough, hoping that the other members would think that the chirping noise was just me, clearing my throat.

Homer chirped again, this time more loudly and insistently. *Uh-oh, it sounds like Homer is getting hungry. I'm glad I brought the medicine dropper.* Our president paused and looked at me suspiciously. "Andrea, are you…chirping?" she asked, raising one eyebrow.

The gig was up. "It's not me; it's Homer," I said, coming clean and opening my palm so that my fellow squad members could see the little sparrow.

"As long as he knows that he's not allowed to vote," our president said with a chuckle.

I dropped Homer off the following morning at the wildlife rehabilitator's home. She told me a few weeks later that Homer was making an excellent recovery and that he was living in a large aviary with many other birds. She planned to return him to the wild when he was ready.

Sometimes first aid calls can be for God's creatures, not just his people. In this case, I was glad I was in the right place at the right time. It may not have made a difference to the bird population in general, but it made a difference to Homer.

....

It was a quiet day at the beach. The gray, overcast skies and threat of rain later in the day were undoubtedly keeping some people at home. I was working as a special officer (better known as a beach cop) at the time and was bicycling along the boardwalk with my partner, Alexa Weiss.

"Pine Cove Dispatch to any special officers in the area of Wesley Avenue Beach," our portable radios suddenly crackled. "We have a report of an injured loon on the beach, possibly covered in oil. Please check it out," Dispatcher Franklin said.

"Received," Alexa responded. "Andrea and I are just a block from there."

"Okay," I said, as we started pumping our mountain bikes toward Wesley Avenue, "I know I live at the beach and all, but what on earth is a loon? I don't think I've ever set eyes on one before."

"I think they're usually too far out to sea to actually see them," Alexa answered. "Honestly, I don't know much about them either, except that they're big with black heads and long, sharp beaks."

"Oh, great," I muttered. "This should be a piece of cake, then." *Did Alexa just say long, sharp beaks?*

Alexa and I parked our bikes near the boardwalk railing at Wesley Avenue and looked out onto the beach. It was easy to spot the location of the call; a small crowd was already forming near the edge of the water. As we jogged across the beach toward the loon, I tried to shrug aside some butterflies that were beginning to flutter in my stomach.

"Andrea, can you see it? That bird is huge!" Alexa exclaimed. "How in the world are we going to catch it without getting bitten?"

"I sure don't remember covering anything like this in specials academy," I said, trying to keep a neutral expression on my face. *Don't let all these bystanders see the fear in your eyes. Act confident. They're counting on us to rescue this bird. We can do this.* At that moment, the loon briefly tried flapping his wings, and I couldn't help but notice how big the wingspan was. *Okay, who am I kidding? I'm scared!*

I studied the loon more closely and began to feel stirrings of sympathy, which were at direct odds with my cowardice. He was covered in what looked to be a dark, oily substance. Even though he was valiantly trying to fly, his wings were not cooperating. A big wave came, pulling him farther out into the water. I knew we were going to have to act quickly, but I was not relishing the prospect of having that long beak clamp down on my skinny forearm. I realized that if we asked the dispatcher to call animal control to help us, it would be too late for the loon. *It looks like it's up to us.* "Alexa, we better grab him quick or he's going to drown," I whispered.

"Yeah," she agreed. "How about I grab the beak, and you grab the body?"

"Are you sure you won't let go?" I asked hesitantly. I could feel the urgency of the crowd behind us, willing us to act.

"Well, I'll try not to," she said.

"Okay, let's do this," I replied. We kicked off our socks and sneakers and tossed them and our radios higher up on the beach, away from the water. Then we stepped into the ocean. I braced myself for what might happen next.

"Now!" Alexa said. She grabbed the loon's head and beak while I threw my arms around his body. It went exactly according to plan… for about one or two seconds.

"I can't hold on!" Alexa yelled as the two of us struggled with the bird and surged more deeply into the ocean waters. Just as she said the words, I saw a huge, angry beak coming straight at my forearm, just as I had feared. I stifled a small scream and then dropped the loon right before it could bite me.

"Oh, this is awful!" I said. "He's going to drown now. We've made it even worse." Instead of struggling in shallow ocean water, now the poor loon was drowning in deeper water. I glanced up toward the beach. The small bunch of onlookers had magically morphed into a much larger crowd, with people watching us from both the beach and from along the boardwalk.

Where did all these onlookers come from? It was so quiet a few minutes ago. I can just see the headlines now: "Special Officers Called to Assist Loon but Killed It Instead."

"Andrea, there are so many people watching now," Alexa said. "We absolutely cannot screw this up. Let's try again. I promise I won't let go this time."

"Okay," I said, feeling the ocean water soak through the bottom of my shorts. We waded more deeply into the waves, our eyes focused on the poor drowning loon.

"Gotcha!" Alexa said, grabbing the beak.

As I grabbed the loon's body, the fireworks began. He began thrashing and struggling for all he was worth. I felt as if I were riding on the back of a mechanical bull, with my body being jerked this way and that. To Alexa's credit, she held true to her word. This time, we were a little more prepared for our feathered friend. However, we must have looked quite a sight, the way the three of us "danced" together in the waves!

After several moments of struggling, the loon calmed down enough for us to work our way out of the surf and back onto the beach.

"Okay, now what do we do with him?" Alexa asked.

I fought back a nervous giggle. We hadn't thought that far ahead. The best thing to do at this point would probably be to radio police headquarters that we caught it and that we needed help. However, neither of us had a free hand to try to pick up our radios.

A friendly middle-aged woman stepped forward from the crowd. "Hi, I'm Mauve Masterson, and I'm a bird lover," she began. "I ran to my car and got this box. Do you think we could put him in here? And I happened to have an old beach towel in the car too. I thought maybe we could wrap him in the beach towel to help calm him down and keep him a little more under control."

"More under control" sounds fantastic right about now.

I kept glancing surreptitiously at Alexa's hand to make sure it remained firmly around the loon's beak. "That sounds like a great idea," I said.

"Okay, then," she replied. "I've already put a bunch of air holes in it." She carefully placed the towel over the bird, and somehow, with some help from the heavens above, we managed to get the irate loon inside the box. As we walked off the beach toward the boardwalk, the crowd of bystanders clapped and cheered.

Thank goodness we were able to rescue the loon. Otherwise, perhaps Alexa and I would have been tarred and feathered ourselves.

"There's a man down south who specializes in rehabilitating aquatic birds, owls, and falcons," Mauve said. "I could drive him there, but I would need someone to hold the box for me. I don't think it would be safe for me to try driving on my own. He might get loose or something."

"Thanks very much for the offer," I replied. "I'll have to check with my boss." After a brief consultation, my boss gave me permission to accompany Mauve in her vehicle for the 30-minute trip. Unfortunately, we hit heavy traffic and it took about an hour to get there. When we finally arrived, the rehabilitation specialist met us at his front door. He was an older gentleman with a long white beard and twinkly blue eyes.

"Hi, I'm Roger," he said, sticking out one wrinkled hand for Mauve to shake. I simply nodded, since I was holding the box with the loon. "Thanks for taking the time to save this fellow. He's quite a big one." He took the loon from us and led us to an attached garage that had been turned into a bird hospital. I glanced around with interest at the numerous owls and vultures rehabilitating in large cages.

We stayed a few minutes and watched as Roger started an IV line on the loon. "He would have never survived if you hadn't brought him in, not with all this oil on his feathers," he said. "He's a pretty sick bird, but don't worry. He's going to be okay."

Then, before I knew it, it was time to say goodbye to Roger and the loon.

Thank you, Lord, for giving Alexa and me the courage not to give up and for letting us play a role in saving one of your blessed creatures.

20

Setting the Stage

Answer me when I call to you,
my righteous God.
Give me relief from my distress;
have mercy on me and hear my prayer.

PSALM 4:1

> **DISPATCHER:** "Request for first aid on Sunset Drive for a pedestrian hit by a car and a woman having a heart attack."

tossed aside the book I was reading and jumped up to answer the call. *I wonder if the woman was driving, hit someone, and then became so upset that she began having some sort of heart problem. It sounds like this might be a bad one.*

Motor vehicle accidents tend to draw out a lot of volunteers, so we were able to roll two ambulances to the call. As we turned the corner onto Sunset Drive, I saw a young girl with long blond hair, lying in the shade of a maple tree, half on the sidewalk and half on the grass. A gray minivan was parked at an odd angle close by. A second girl with short dark hair stood clutching her chest and pointing at the girl on the sidewalk.

Have both girls been struck by a car? Or was the girl on the sidewalk hit and her friend is just very upset?

When I looked more closely, I noticed that farther down on the sidewalk, about 15 feet away, a third girl was holding a camcorder. "Why does that girl have a video camera?" I asked. "She looks like she's filming everything that's happening."

When my fellow first aid squad members and I jumped out of the ambulances, the girl on the sidewalk jumped to her feet. The girl who had been clutching her chest let her arms slowly sink down to her sides. They no longer looked either sick or injured, and both looked at us sheepishly.

"Do you girls need help?" I asked, already guessing what their answer would be.

"No," they said in unison, as they gathered their belongings and started to back away from us.

"We received a call for a person hit by a car and a person having a heart attack at this location," I said.

"Oh," one of the girls said. "I think I can explain. It's all a mistake. We're filming a movie for a school project. We're really sorry if we caused any trouble."

We later learned that a passing motorist had thought the girls were in distress and so called 911. Luckily, it turned out to be a misunderstanding.

....

Chester Kelly gently tapped his brakes as he negotiated a curve in the road. On his way to his doctor's appointment an hour earlier, he'd passed what looked like a car accident involving some young girls. He saw ambulances and police cars, so he figured they were getting the help they needed. Chester was almost 85, and it always upset him to see young people who were ill or injured.

Chester's mind flashed ahead to the rest of the evening. He decided he would stop at the deli on his way home and grab a turkey sandwich for dinner. He hated cooking, because his fingers weren't as nimble as they used to be. Sometimes, he struggled just to open cans and jars.

He continued driving, pausing briefly for a squirrel that ran in front of his car. Knowing he had the right of way at the upcoming intersection, he resumed the speed limit and proceeded along. He suddenly realized that a red van was coming quickly toward him from the west. He knew instinctively that it wasn't going to stop at the stop sign. He heard the loud squealing of tires but knew that the van's driver would never be able to stop in time to avoid hitting him. Too late to have a real chance to react, Chester nevertheless attempted to swerve out of the way. He grunted as the van slammed into the front passenger side of his car. He felt his head snap sideways and his knees smash against the steering wheel. A tearing sensation lit through his back, setting it aflame with a burning pain. *Dear Lord, please help me!*

....

"It's supposed to start raining tonight," my dad said as he poured himself a glass of milk.

"Yeah, I heard. That will probably spoil our plans to go for ice cream and a stroll on the boardwalk." Just as I finished what I was saying, a tremendous bang sounded close to our home.

"Must be an accident at the corner," my dad said, hurriedly placing the milk carton down on the counter. The two of us rushed out the front door and down the street. I winced at the sight: A red van had deeply intruded into the front passenger side of a navy-blue sedan. It looked as though the van had blown the stop sign, though it was hard to know for sure. A young man stood by the driver's seat of the van, leaning on the doorframe. "I'm okay," he yelled to us. "But I think he needs help," he added, pointing toward the blue car.

As we reached the sedan, I spotted an elderly man hunched over the steering wheel. His eyes were closed, and he was motionless. "Dad, please go home and call the police. Tell them we need first aid." My father nodded his head and quickly retraced his steps.

I looked around and made sure the accident scene was safe. There were no electrical wires touching the cars and no signs of a fire. I tapped the driver's side window and opened the door. "Sir," I began. "My name is Andrea, and I'm on the rescue squad. What's your name?"

The gentleman stirred and opened his eyes. "Chester," he said weakly. "Chester Kelly."

"Mr. Kelly, does anything hurt? Are you having any chest pain or trouble breathing?" Despite the severity of the impact, his airbag had not deployed, possibly because of the side-impact collision.

"My back," Mr. Kelly replied. "The pain is terrible." I noticed how pale he was. I placed my fingers on the side of his wrist to check his radial pulse. *Weak and rapid. He's not looking so good.*

"Mr. Kelly, I'm going to climb into the car behind you, and I'm going to hold your head and neck still until the rest of the rescue squad gets here, okay?" He nodded his head, so I slid in behind him and placed my hands on either side of his head. Since he had very little hair, I could feel the clamminess of his scalp beneath my fingers. "Where do you live?" I asked, trying to assess his cognitive status.

Mr. Kelly murmured his address. He lived only a couple miles away on the other side of town. "My back's hurting really bad," he whispered. "Will the ambulance be here soon?" Just as he was asking the question, my pager went off.

DISPATCHER: "Request for first aid at the intersection of Meade and Fourth for a motor vehicle accident with two injuries."

"About two minutes," I replied. "Do you have any medical problems?" I knew if the answer was yes, it could place Chester at greater risk for complications.

"Actually, I just left the doctor's office. I had a checkup and got a few of my medications adjusted. I've had a couple heart attacks and mini-strokes in the past," he said.

A couple of heart attacks. He may need oxygen when the rig gets here.

"Anything else?" I prompted.

"Well, I was just diagnosed a few weeks ago with an aneurysm," he said.

"Where exactly is the aneurysm?" I asked, shifting my hands slightly.

"It's an abdominal aortic aneurysm," he murmured. "I'm getting my pre-op bloodwork and testing done. I'm supposed to have surgery in a week or so. The doc said that it's like a ticking time bomb and that I need to get it taken care of sooner rather than later."

My blood suddenly ran cold. I was thrust back in time to a Thanksgiving Day several years earlier when we had two calls for an elderly gentleman. On the first call, he simply complained of a flare-up of his chronic back pain. The emergency room sent him home with pain pills, but the pain became progressively worse. When we brought him back to the emergency room later that same evening, he was diagnosed with a ruptured abdominal aortic aneurysm, also called an AAA. The doctor said that the AAA was most likely inoperable and thought that the gentleman had only a very short time to live.

Has Mr. Kelly's AAA ruptured? Or is the pain orthopedic in nature and due to the car accident?

"What does the back pain feel like?" I asked, glad to hear police and first aid sirens in the distance.

"Excruciating," Chester said after a long pause. "Like my back is literally being torn in two."

"Does it feel like it's throbbing over your belly button?" I asked, shifting my knees to the side in the cramped rear of the car.

"Yes, you could say that. It's bad, isn't it?" he asked. "Please be honest."

"Well, the doctors are going to need to do a lot of tests to make sure everything is okay," I hedged. I knew the situation might be serious, but I certainly didn't want to panic him.

"You're worried about my aneurysm, aren't you?" he guessed.

"I am concerned, yes. It looks like you and your car took quite a hit. But you'll be in good hands at the hospital," I said, relieved to see Alec, Dillon, and Meg stepping out of one of our ambulances and heading toward us.

"I'm in good hands already," Chester said. "The Lord's hands. I made that choice a long time ago."

"Then everything will turn out all right," I said simply.

Faith. One small word with such vast implications. I knew that faith in Jesus would carry Mr. Kelly through this crisis. He would be okay, whatever the outcome might turn out to be.

Meg performed an assessment on Chester while Dillon placed a cervical collar around his neck. "We'll skip the KED," Meg said. "Let's go straight for the backboard." Since the KED, or Kendrick Extrication Device, is time consuming to apply, we skip it in cases that require rapid extrication. Alec slid a backboard underneath Chester's bottom, and we carefully maneuvered him onto it. Since the edge of the backboard was already resting on the stretcher, we were then able to slide Chester the rest of the way onto the stretcher and quickly strap him in.

As we loaded him into the ambulance, paramedics Rose and William arrived. Dillon offered to drive their ambulance so they could both ride in the back of ours with Chester. Alec slipped into the driver's seat of our rig, so Meg and I hopped into the back with Chester. I'm not sure if it was my imagination or the lighting, but Chester seemed to be looking paler by the minute. Meg and I filled William and Rose in on his condition. When I mentioned the aneurysm, William immediately flipped up Chester's shirt to see for himself. I tried not to grimace at the sight: an obvious pulsating mass close to Chester's umbilicus.

Rose called ahead to the emergency room and explained what was going on. I could tell from her facial expression and tone of voice that she was worried about the aneurysm too. All of us knew that the clock was running and that each minute was vitally important. "Blood pressure is falling," William said tersely.

I reached over and held Chester's hand to comfort him while I checked his pulse. *Still weak.* "How are you feeling, Mr. Kelly?" I asked.

"Not so great, I'm afraid. In fact, I'm starting to feel really cold." I placed another blanket on top of him and draped another over the top of his head and around his shoulders. Within a few minutes, our ambulance was backing into a parking place at the emergency room.

The triage nurse, Maggie, met us in the hallway. "Right this way," she said briskly as she led us to one of the triage rooms. The emergency room physician was already waiting for us. Dr. Parnell, a top-notch doctor in her field, sensed the urgency of the situation. "Mr. Kelly," she said, "I've already studied your medical records on the computer. I've called your surgeon, and he's on his way here. In the meantime, I'm going to run a few tests. I just want you to know that there's a chance that he may be performing your aneurysm surgery today instead of next week as originally planned."

Chester nodded his head weakly. "Do whatever you need to do, Doc."

"We'll all be thinking of you," Meg said as we gathered our equipment.

"That's what I need," Chester said softly. "Prayers. Thanks."

I squeezed his hand briefly and headed into the hallway with my fellow members. We were all somber, knowing the serious situation he faced. I reminded myself of Chester's own words: *"I'm in good hands, the Lord's hands."* If he could have faith, then so could I.

A week later, I noticed Chester's name in the church bulletin under the "Pray for the Sick" list. My face broke into a smile. *Chester's name is listed under the sick list and not the deceased list!* If Chester had undergone surgery for the aneurysm, he must have survived it! A month later, our squad received a thank-you note from Chester:

> Dear First Aid Squad Members,
>
> Thank you for your care and kindness during my accident last month. I thought you might like to know that I underwent emergency surgery because my aneurysm had started leaking. I made a full recovery and am back to puttering around in my garden. Enclosed is a check to show my heartfelt appreciation.
>
> Sincerely,
> Chester Kelly

I was thrilled to learn that Chester had such a wonderful outcome. I learned a valuable lesson from him the day of the accident, witnessing firsthand how he put his faith into action.

21

Murder!

Those who walk righteously and speak what is right,
who reject gain from extortion
and keep their hands from accepting bribes,
who stop their ears against plots of murder and shut their
eyes against contemplating evil—
they are the ones who will dwell on the heights, whose
refuge will be the mountain fortress.
Their bread will be supplied, and water will not fail them.

ISAIAH 33:15-16

Happy Birthday!" Skeeter McGuire said, pulling his wife, Helen, into his arms. Skeeter had been a volunteer with the Pine Cove Fire Department for even longer than Helen had been on the first aid squad. This weekend, they had decided to take a mini-vacation to celebrate Helen's birthday. Helen's mother was watching their kids for the night, giving them a chance to have a getaway at the Pine Cove Hotel.

The evening began with a romantic dinner for two in the hotel restaurant. Helen enjoyed prime rib with mashed potatoes while Skeeter savored a dish of veal parmesan. As dearly as she loved her children, Helen was enjoying being able to converse with her husband without little voices piping in and interrupting every few minutes.

Now, after a lovely evening in each other's company, Helen and Skeeter were ready to call it a night. Helen took off her first aid pager and placed it in its recharger, which she had already plugged into an outlet and placed on the hotel's night table. Skeeter did the same with his fire department pager. Being dedicated volunteers, the pair had brought their pagers with them for their night away. As they drifted off to sleep, neither could have guessed what the night still had in store for them.

....

The shrill ringing of the telephone yanked Luis Gonzales from his reverie. He glanced at the caller ID but opted not to pick up the phone. Juan Ramirez had called numerous times over the past several weeks, but Luis dared not speak with him. He knew that it was way too dangerous. Speaking to Juan now could foil his plan and ruin everything.

Luis opened the top drawer of his nightstand, pushed a few old magazines, a cigarette lighter, and some stained corks out of the way, and dug out an old, worn eyeglass case. He carefully unzipped the case and pulled out a sizeable wad of money. With sweaty fingertips, he counted the cash. *So much money! Twelve hundred and one dollars. All the things my family and I can do with twelve hundred dollars.* Luis brushed aside the brief stab of guilt that it wasn't really all his.

Luis found his mind wandering back to the summer. He and Juan had been roommates, sharing a basement room of the Pine Cove Hotel. They worked as dish cleaners in the hotel's kitchen. Neither of them was in the country legally, so Luis tried to keep a low profile. Juan was not so fortunate. He ticked off their boss, and he ended up getting fired.

Juan had asked Luis to safeguard his savings of $750 so that it would be protected in case of an "emergency." Luis willingly agreed, and at first, he was true to his word. But after Juan moved to Brooklyn, Luis found himself starting to think of the $750 as his own and not Juan's.

Seven hundred and fifty dollars is a lot of money, especially back home.

As Juan's phone calls became more persistent, Luis had developed a plan. He used some of the money to buy an airline ticket to fly back to his own country. In the morning, he would fly home, give the money to his family, and lie low for a while. Hopefully, before long, Juan would forget all about him and his $750.

....

Juan Ramirez's knuckles turned white from clenching the phone as he listened to it ring and ring. In frustration, he finally slammed the cordless handpiece on its receiver. He'd been calling Luis Gonzales for weeks. He wanted his money back—now! He didn't trust Luis anymore, and he berated himself for ever trusting his old roommate with his hard-earned money in the first place. A week ago, he'd heard a rumor that Luis was planning to return to Mexico before Christmas.

Earlier today, he'd learned that Luis would be catching a seven a.m. flight tomorrow! He was sure in the very depths of his gut that Luis Gonzales would be boarding that plane with his $750 in his pocket. The thought burned Juan to the core. There was no way he was going to stand by and let that happen. He wasn't going to let Luis run off with his cash.

Juan wasn't a warm and fuzzy kind of guy. He blamed that on his father, who had beaten him pretty much every day of his childhood until one day, when his father finally took off and never came back. As a result, Juan found it extremely hard to care about anyone. His personal motto was to suspect everyone and trust no one. So far, he wasn't thrilled with the way his life was going.

Juan glanced at the old clock on the apartment wall. *Just before midnight. I still have time!* Juan yanked open the rotting pine kitchen cabinet, ignoring the rusty hinges that were practically falling off. Pushing aside containers of salt, pepper, and oregano, he pulled out his .357 Magnum and stuck it in the waistband of his pants. Next, he jerked open a creaky kitchen drawer and pulled out his sharpest knife. The handle was slightly loose and the blade a bit rusty, but it would have to do. Grabbing the phone again, he dialed the number of one of his closest acquaintances.

"Alonso, do you remember that problem I told you about? Well, I need your help. I'll be over in ten minutes," Juan said with a steely voice. *It's time to take action.*

....

"Don't worry, Rosita," Luis said to his girlfriend as he draped his arm around her shoulders. "I'll be back in six months. The time will fly by. You'll see."

Rosita shifted so that she faced Luis directly. She placed her hands on his waist, pulling him closer. "I'll hold you to that," she murmured, resting her soft cheek against his stubbly one.

A sudden loud knocking at the hotel room door startled Luis, and he quickly pulled away from Rosita. He glanced at the digital clock on the end table. *Four o'clock. My flight leaves at seven. My cab will be here within the hour, and I can finally stop worrying.* Luis tapped Rosita's shoulder and held a finger to his lips, motioning her to remain quiet and still.

The banging became louder and more insistent. Luis wondered if the wood might start splintering or give way from the force. "Open up, Luis! I know you're in there!"

Luis broke into a cold sweat, with rivulets of moisture dripping between his shoulder blades and down the center of his back. He'd recognize that voice anywhere.

Juan! He must have found out I'm leaving. What do I do? He briefly fingered the old eyeglass case in his rear jeans pocket. *I'm keeping the money, no matter what. It's mine now!*

"Open the door, Luis! I want my money back," Juan bellowed. "I am not a patient man!" Juan began jiggling the doorknob. It was locked, but Luis knew that was merely a temporary inconvenience. What he didn't know was that when Juan was fired over the summer, he hadn't bothered to return his key. Within moments, the door was unlocked and yanked wide open.

Rosita cowered behind the sofa, her breaths becoming shallow and rapid as her eyes widened with fear. Luis found himself slowly backing up, trying to put as much distance as possible between Juan and himself. There was only one door out of here, and Juan and his goon-friend Alonso had it effectively blocked. Alonso had visited Juan several times over the summer, even crashing in their room for a few nights. At the time, Luis had found Alonso's cold, hard stares and mean disposition disturbing, but he hadn't been directly on the receiving end of them back then. Now, he found them downright terrifying. *I need to get out of here!*

"I don't have your money!" Luis exclaimed, suddenly rushing forward toward the door. He darted around Alonso and shoved Juan. *If I can just make it five doors down the hall…*

Luis tore down the hallway toward his nephew's and brother-in-law's room. *They'll help me out of this mess.* Frantically, he jerked the door open and rushed inside. "It's Juan," he shouted. "He's after me!"

Juan charged into the room after Luis and pulled his gleaming .357 Magnum from his waistband. "You give me my money back right now, and no one has to get hurt, okay?" he yelled, waving the gun at the three men. Alonso entered and stood behind Juan, brandishing the butcher knife Juan had brought from his kitchen.

I need to get that gun before he kills me! Luis charged forward, desperately grabbing for the gun. Enraged, Juan flung his arm back and then swung it forward with tremendous force and precision, smashing the gun against Luis's skull.

Luis staggered from the sheer force of the blow, fearful that he might pass out from the excruciating pain. *I can't pass out. If I do, he'll surely take the money.* Luis blinked a few times and shook his head to clear the sudden fogginess. *I…must…get out of here.* He half-lunged, half-stumbled forward and back into the hallway, willing his legs to cooperate. *Run, run!* Luis sprinted down the hallway, subconsciously holding his breath. His eyes glazed over as he focused on one thing: running for his life.

"Stop!" Juan ordered, cursing loudly as he chased Luis down the hall.

Luis heard Juan's steps getting closer until he could almost feel Juan's hot breath on the nape of his neck. He briefly felt something hard brush up against the center of his back. *Dear God, I hope that's not Juan's gun I feel!* Then, just as he thought Juan would tackle him to the ground, he heard a loud popping noise. Almost simultaneously, a burning, searing pain tore straight through his back clear to the front of his chest. Luis crumpled to the ground, desperately struggling to get air into his lungs.

Juan uttered an expletive and, together with Alonso, they bolted down the hallway. The pair then silently slipped out of the Pine Cove Hotel and away into the darkness.

Rosita and Luis's relatives rushed down the hallway and knelt next to him. Rosita cradled Luis's head in her hands as her tears spilled down her cheeks and onto his. "He shot me, Rosita," Luis whispered, struggling to get the words out. "Juan shot me." Luis felt an odd floating sensation and closed his eyes.

Rosita began screaming, her piercing wails emanating throughout the hallway. "Help, help us," she sobbed. "I don't know what to do. Luis has been shot!"

"I love you," Luis whispered. "I'm so sorry." His body became still as he drew his last breath.

....

DISPATCHER: "Request for first aid in the basement of the Pine Cove Hotel for a gunshot wound."

Helen sat bolt upright in her hotel bed and jumped to her feet, all in one fluid motion. Her husband, Skeeter, did the same. "Did the dispatcher just say what I think he said?" Skeeter asked with disbelief. "A gunshot wound? Right here in the basement of our hotel?"

"Yes," Helen replied as she quickly pulled on a shirt and pair of pants. "What are the odds?" *Could it be some sort of accident? Or is this a prank?*

"Maybe someone was trying to clean their gun," Skeeter suggested as the pair rushed toward the door.

"Or maybe self-inflicted?" Helen suggested. "I'm not even sure how to get to the basement!"

"Follow me. I know how to get there!" Skeeter exclaimed. "We'll take the stairs." Even though they were staying on the fourth floor, he reasoned that the stairs would be faster than the elevator. The pair sprinted down the hall, their footsteps almost noiseless on the plush mauve carpeting. They entered the stairwell, and soon the sound of their pounding feet filled the air. Helen grabbed the railing, mentally checking off each time they passed a different floor. *One flight, two flights, three flights, four flights, almost there!*

They burst through the stairwell door into the basement, rushed across a small lounge area, and swung open the door to where the hotel employees lived. A scene of confusion and pandemonium was unfolding before them. As they crossed the threshold, Helen and Skeeter ran directly into about eight people who were yelling with great excitement. Helen wasn't sure what they were saying because they weren't speaking English.

Helen hesitated for a moment in the doorway, and was relieved to spot Officer Fred Smith just a few feet away. Officer Smith, an extremely experienced law enforcement officer, was approaching retirement. "You two have just entered a crime scene," he said and jotted both their names and the exact time directly on the wall near where they stood. "Follow me."

Helen squeezed past a short woman with dark hair held back in a loose ponytail. Tears streamed down her face as she waved her arms in the air, seemingly recounting what had just happened. An older man wearing a white tank top and faded black sweatpants stood in front of her, listening to her story.

Officer Smith led Helen and Skeeter down the length of the hallway to a spot near an exit door. "There's the victim," he said, pointing to a figure who lay facedown on the floor. His right hand was gripping what looked to Helen to be an eyeglass case. A small bullet hole was visible in the center of his back. Apparently, a bullet had torn right through his coat and lodged somewhere in his body. *Murder!*

"He's gone," Officer Smith said. "I already checked before you got here. No pulse. You can see the entrance wound on his back. I couldn't find an exit wound."

Helen glanced over her shoulder at all the people milling about the hallway. *Could one of these people possibly be the killer?*

Officer Smith pulled his radio from its holster. "Make sure you have an interpreter coming," he directed the dispatcher. "Have the first aid stand by outside. We're not going to be needing them in here."

As EMS workers, we are called to save lives. It's quite difficult to accept that there are cases in which absolutely nothing can be done for the person.

Helen gazed at the murder victim, wishing there was something, anything, she could do to help. She realized this poor man had already passed from his life on earth. It struck her how just hours earlier, she was celebrating her own day of birth while this poor gentleman was spending what would turn out to be his last day.

....

The next day

Christmas was only a few weeks away. I was busy studying for my college semester exams and looking forward to being able to go home for the holidays. Ready for a study break, I decided to call Helen and wish her a happy birthday. She picked up on the second ring.

"Happy birthday!" I exclaimed. "How was your weekend get-away?"

"You'll never guess what happened yesterday…" she began.

....

Two days later

Juan's chest felt tight, and he struggled to get a deep breath in. Despite the cold air, sweat dripped down the front of his chest into the waistband of his pants. *It's just nerves. I'll be fine once I get my gun back.* Three nights earlier, after Juan shot Luis, he had raced from the Pine Cove Hotel down to the beach and hidden the .357 Magnum under the boardwalk. He hadn't had much time, but he managed to bury it under a piece of driftwood, some empty soda cans, and an old greasy pizza box.

Now Juan found himself back at the beach again and wishing that he were somewhere else, preferably far, far away. He had gotten himself into this terrible mess, all for $750 dollars, which he never even got back from Luis. How he wished he had his money back! He had only meant to scare Luis, but somehow things had gotten totally out of hand.

As Juan approached the boardwalk, he worried that he might not remember exactly where he had hidden his gun, or worse yet, that someone else might have already found it. He quickened his pace, looked furtively to the left and right, and then darted underneath the boardwalk. Holding his breath, he knelt in the spot where he had hidden his gun and anxiously lifted the pizza box. With relief, his eyes rested on the muzzle of his gun, peeking out from a foot-long piece of driftwood and still pressed up against an empty soda can. Juan grabbed the gun and shoved it into his coat pocket. *I made it!*

....

Rico ambled aimlessly along the boardwalk, mourning the loss of his Uncle Luis. He paused and placed both hands on the boardwalk railing as he stared out at the ocean. The large waves relentlessly pounded the shoreline, much the same way Rico imagined he'd like to pound his fist into Juan Ramirez's pockmarked face.

Rico bitterly regretted that Juan had managed to slip away after shooting his uncle. He'd briefly considered running after him, but he knew he was no match for Juan's gun. A group of police officers had come right away, but Juan had already disappeared like a card from a magician's deck.

The events from three nights ago repeatedly replayed in Rico's head. How he would love to get his hands on Juan! Breaking his gaze from the ocean, he turned to continue walking. He suddenly froze in his tracks as he stared at the profile of a familiar figure standing about 20 yards away, illuminated by a streetlamp. He would know that profile anywhere. It was Juan!

Rico fought back the strong urge to rush over and confront Juan. He realized that Juan could very well still be packing heat. Rico most certainly did not want to end up like his uncle. Instead, he stealthily slipped off the boardwalk and rushed across the street to a payphone. His hand shaking slightly, he dialed for the operator.

"How can I help you?" the operator asked.

"This is an emergency. Connect me to the Pine Cove Police Department right away!" Rico could only pray Juan would still be there when the police arrived.

....

The police did indeed arrest Juan Ramirez that night. He was carrying a .357 Magnum that still had five cartridges in its six-cartridge chamber. A state police ballistics expert found that the bullet removed from Luis Gonzalez's body had been fired from Juan's gun. An autopsy revealed that when Juan struck Luis in the head with his gun, he fractured Luis's skull. Juan was subsequently charged with murder, felony murder, aggravated assault, and possession of a weapon for an unlawful purpose.

Juan claimed that he'd slipped while running and had accidentally fired his gun. Nevertheless, the jury found him guilty on all counts and sentenced him to death. Upon appeal, the convictions were affirmed, though the death penalty was reversed. Although his life was spared, I reflected that Juan lost his freedom due to a moment of passion. Two lives essentially lost, all over a stolen $750.

22

Tears from Heaven

I will praise the LORD, who counsels me;
even at night my heart instructs me.
I keep my eyes always on the LORD.
With him at my right hand, I will not be shaken.

PSALM 16:7-8

Emma Sutton desperately wanted to be popular. She longed to be part of the "in" crowd. So, when a classmate suggested that she raid her parents' liquor cabinet, she gladly did. It was easy, really. She had known for a long time where her parents hid the key. She waited until she had a few minutes alone and crammed as much wine, vodka, and gin into her backpack as she could. She tried to shake aside the feelings of guilt that nagged at her conscience.

It'll be okay. They'll never even notice it's missing. I need to do this. The other kids will think I'm so cool when I show them how much I got. She tried to ignore the fact that she had always been a good, honest kid and that her parents trusted her completely.

Except for a sip of champagne at her cousin's wedding last year, Emma had never tasted alcohol. After all, she was only 15 years old. Still, when her classmates suggested that she meet them in the woods behind the field where the town was having a bluegrass concert that evening, Emma was thrilled. The next thing she knew, they were all laughing and having such a good time. For the first time, Emma felt popular. *I hope this feeling lasts forever!*

Somewhere deep within, she knew she was probably drinking too much, too fast. But at that moment, Emma didn't care.

When the liquor was all gone and the other kids got up to leave, Emma realized she couldn't get up. A few of them tried to pull her to her feet, but her legs felt like jelly and wouldn't cooperate. "Just sleep it off, Emma," she thought she heard someone say. Everything started spinning, and she felt as though she was going to throw up. Emma decided to rest on the ground for a few minutes until the terrible spinning sensation went away. She was vaguely aware that pine needles were poking into her cheek, but it didn't seem to matter.

....

In the days when I was working as a special officer for the police department, my boss asked me to stay a few extra hours and stand by at a local bluegrass concert. It was an easy assignment. I merely needed to stroll around and be present in case someone needed assistance. It was a perfect summer evening with just a hint of a gentle sea breeze. I figured there would be mainly an older crowd at the concert, relaxing in their beach chairs and enjoying the music. I was looking forward to enjoying the music myself. And I did. That is, for about a half hour, until dusk.

I decided to take a walk along the tree line and make sure all was quiet. Nothing much ever happens in our town, so I honestly wasn't expecting to find anything or anyone out of the ordinary. I headed toward the trees, my new sneakers squeaking on the damp grass. Suddenly, an odd noise caught my attention and the hairs on the back of my neck stood up. I felt ill at ease. I took my police radio out of its holster and held it in my hand, just in case I should need it.

I'm being silly. It's probably just a squirrel.

I paused and stood still, listening for the strange noise again. And then…there it was…heavy breathing followed by a soft moan. *Stop being a chicken. March over toward the noise and figure out what it is and where it's coming from.*

I strained my eyes to better see into the darkness. *I sure wish I had brought a flashlight.*

My heart thudding, I followed the sounds of the heavy breathing deeper into the trees. I glanced back, reassured by the knowledge that if I needed help, I could scream loud enough for the people at the concert to be able to hear me. The breathing was getting louder and louder, so I knew I was getting closer. *There's someone or something under that bush.*

I took a deep breath and forced myself to get closer. I could see short, skinny legs protruding at an odd angle from the bush. I pushed a few branches out of the way to see more clearly. *Why, it's a young girl!*

The unconscious girl was lying facedown, her face pushed against the base of the evergreen bush. Long blond hair cascaded across part of her face, tangled with some of the lower branches of the bush. Taking care to stabilize her neck and spine, I rolled her onto her side to make sure that she had a clear airway. She looked quite young, maybe 15 or 16 years old at the most.

"Hey, are you okay?" I asked. She didn't respond to my question, so I gently tapped her shoulder. She was completely unresponsive.

How could such a young girl be unconscious? I didn't have to wonder very long, for I found an empty vodka bottle underneath her. It was time to call the police department for help.

"I need the first aid and patrols in the woods behind the concert for an unconscious female with possible alcohol poisoning," I radioed to the dispatcher.

Within minutes, Officer Sims arrived, flashlight in hand. "How's she doing?" he asked, kneeling on the ground next to me.

"She's in pretty bad shape. Totally unresponsive," I replied, pulling a few more strands of her hair out of a low-hanging branch. "Her heart rate is 60 and regular, and her respirations are 14. I can't get a blood pressure yet because I don't have a cuff with me."

"I recognize her," Officer Sims said. "Her name is Emma Sutton. She's going into tenth grade, I think. I'll radio dispatch to contact her parents and let them know we're taking her to the hospital."

Just then, Colleen, Ted, and Archie arrived. I filled them in on what was going on. "I'm so glad you brought that emesis basin. I'm afraid that we're going to need to use it really soon." I could barely finish my sentence. Although Emma was still unconscious, she began heaving and spraying vomit. I was wearing shorts and tried to dodge it as best as I could, but grimaced when I realized that a few drops landed on my new sneakers. I knew it was a good thing for Emma's sake that she was vomiting, because it would help to get some of the alcohol out of her system.

Colleen, Archie, and Ted took Emma to the hospital. Since I was still working, I stayed behind at the concert. We found out later that Emma had a life-threatening blood alcohol level. Alcohol can cause low blood sugar, seizures, and coma in children. Fortunately, Emma made a full recovery. She was truly blessed that I happened upon her when I did. Without the life-saving treatment provided by the emergency room staff, she could have easily lost her life that evening…from a bottle of vodka.

....

Final exams are finally over. It feels so wonderful! Carly Desimone wanted to let out a whoop of joy, but she was starting to feel kind of queasy. She and her friends Isabella, Mike, and Logan were celebrating the end of the college semester and the beginning of summer by barhopping. They started at about six o'clock, and now, some seven hours later, Carly was starting to feel the effects of so much liquor. She blinked and looked around, temporarily confused.

Where am I? Oh, that's right. The cab driver is taking us to another bar. Can't remember which one though.

She was starting to wish she hadn't drunk so much and was wondering if she was going to have a terrible hangover in the morning. But right now, she was more concerned that she needed some fresh air. She fumbled with the side of the door but couldn't figure out which button controlled the window. *Why won't my fingers cooperate with me?*

"I need some air," she said softly. No one seemed to hear her. An old rock song was playing on the car radio. Isabella and Mike were singing along, oblivious to the fact they were off-key. Carly glanced sideways, toward the rear middle seat of their cab. Logan must have passed out at some point, because he was now leaning heavily on her. Suddenly feeling claustrophobic, Carly pushed Logan away. His weight shifted to the other side of the car, onto Isabella.

"I need some fresh air," Carly said a little louder. Still, none of her friends heard her. Almost desperate at this point, she fiddled with the buttons on the car door. Then, much to her relief, the window suddenly lowered. Carly stuck her head out the window and breathed deeply. *It's not enough. I'm going to throw up. I need more air!* Almost in a trance, she swung her arms out of the window, grabbing the upper frame of the car. Years of gymnastics training took over, and Carly deftly pulled her upper body out of the car. Then she pushed off with her feet and scrambled onto the car's roof. *Finally, some fresh air.*

....

Mia Cosgrove tapped on her steering wheel with her thumbs, humming along with her car radio. She had made some decent tips working as a waitress tonight, and now she was looking forward to a good night's sleep before doing it all over again tomorrow night.

An odd movement in the car in front of her caught her attention. A wave of goose bumps suddenly arose upon the nape of her neck. *Please tell me that's not a person climbing onto the roof of the car in front of me. Are they crazy?* Peering more closely, she caught a flash of a long, dark ponytail as the car passed under a streetlight. Filled with panic, Mia fumbled to get her cell phone out of her purse and dialed 911.

"Pine Grove Police," Dispatcher Jerome Franklin said.

"Help!" Mia yelled, fighting back a wave of rising hysteria. "There's a girl on the roof of the car in front of me and she's barely holding on. I'm afraid she's going to fall off. You have to help her!"

"I'll send the patrols there immediately. Where are you right now?" Dispatcher Franklin asked.

"I'm on Bergen Street," Mia said, her voice trembling.

"Are you heading north or south? Can you give me a cross street?"

"South. I'm not sure about a cross street, but I just passed the ice cream parlor," she said. "I'm so afraid she's going to fall. This road is really bumpy. What should I do? Should I beep my horn to try to stop them? Should I pull up next to them? But what if she falls off and I run her over by accident?"

"Just try to stay calm and drive slowly behind them," Dispatcher Franklin advised. "Remain on the line in case we need more information."

"Oh no! She fell off!" Mia slammed on her brakes and threw her car into park. She jumped out and rushed to the young woman, who now lay unmoving near the side of the road.

I need to stay calm if I want to be able to help her. I hope she's okay.

Mia squatted down near the young woman and shuddered when she saw a pool of dark red blood already forming around her head. Fighting back a wave of nausea, she said, "Miss, are you okay?" *She's not answering me at all. Is she dead? Oh, please tell me she's not dead.* Mia looked up with relief to see two police cars arriving on the scene. "The car kept going," she said between sobs once the officers approached them. "I don't think they even know she fell off their roof." She pointed in the direction the car was traveling. Wordlessly, Officer Endicott jumped back in his patrol car and took off.

Officer Sims knelt next to the victim and checked for a pulse. "Weak carotid," he muttered. Grabbing his portable radio, he said to Dispatcher Franklin, "Have the first aid squad step it up. Tell them to expedite. Patient is unresponsive with a severe head injury."

....

DISPATCHER: "Request for first aid on Bergen Street—in front of the ice cream parlor—for a severe head injury. Possible fall from the roof of a moving car. Expedite."

Alec, Helen, Meg, Buddy, and I climbed into the ambulance. "Did the dispatcher say what I think he said?" Buddy asked, shaking his head in disbelief. "A fall off the roof of a moving car? Sounds very strange to me."

"That's what he said," Meg replied, grabbing the trauma kit off a shelf in the rear of the ambulance. "I guess we'll find out in about one minute for sure."

"The medics have a ten-minute ETA," I said, donning a pair of gloves. "It sounds like we're going to need them."

As we pulled up closer to the accident scene, Officer Sims pointed to where we should park the ambulance. The first thing I heard was the sound of sobbing, but at a glance I could tell that it wasn't coming from our patient. I looked toward the curb and saw a young woman with short curly hair, her head in her hands, crying uncontrollably.

Officer Sims caught the direction of my glance. "She saw her fall off the roof, and she's very shaken up," he explained. "From what we can gather, the patient's name is Carly Desimone, but we're working on confirming that."

Our team knelt around Carly, wordlessly doing what we knew had to be done. Helen held cervical stabilization with a modified jaw thrust in case Carly had a neck injury. Buddy strapped a non-rebreather mask around her face to provide high-flow oxygen. I shined a flashlight onto Carly for Meg, so she could better check vital signs and perform a head-to-toe assessment.

"There seems to be a depressed spot in her skull—she may have a skull fracture," Meg said as she carefully palpated Carly's scalp and face. "And it feels like there's a loose flap of skin on the back of her head. We'll be able to see it better when we roll her on her side for the backboard."

I noticed the copious amount of dark, sticky blood pooling underneath Carly's head. I passed a large trauma dressing to Alec with my free hand. When we rolled her to her side to check her spine and the back of her head, Alec carefully placed the dressing onto the injured area. "Better hand me another just in case. It's bleeding heavily."

"Open your eyes, Carly," Meg said, but her eyes remained closed.

"Can you squeeze my hand?" Again, Carly didn't respond, but instead lay completely motionless.

"What's her Glasgow score?" Helen asked, shifting her hands a bit as Alec placed a cervical collar around Carly's neck. "A three?"

"Yes, a three," Meg replied.

The Glasgow Coma Scale measures a patient's best eye, motor, and verbal response. A score of 15 is the best, and 3 is the worst. We all knew that Carly's situation was extremely critical.

Dear Lord, please be with Carly right now as she battles for her life.

We finished securing Carly to our backboard and lifted it onto our stretcher just as a yellow cab rolled up. An ashen-faced young woman jumped out and rushed over. "I didn't know," she said frantically. "I didn't know she was on the roof. I don't understand. Carly, it's me, Isabella. Wake up!"

My gut clenched at the profound sadness of the scene unfolding before us. As a physical therapist, I knew that Carly had possibly sustained a very severe traumatic brain injury and perhaps a skull fracture. Even if she survived, she might never be herself again. I didn't want to think of the possibility that she could remain in a persistent vegetative state.

"We're taking her to the hospital," Buddy said kindly. "If you don't mind, we need to ask you a few questions about your friend."

"Of course," Isabella said, trying to take a few deep breaths to calm down. "What do you need to know?"

"Can you tell us what happened tonight?" Buddy asked.

"We were celebrating the end of final exams," Isabella explained, her voice shaking. "We went out to a bunch of different places. It was quite loud in the car, between the radio and everyone singing. None of us noticed that she got out of the car."

"Do you know if she has any medical problems?" Buddy prompted, as he jotted down Isabella's answers.

"No, not that I know of." Isabella sighed. "I just feel like suddenly I've been thrown into some horrible nightmare, like this can't really be happening. Carly's my best friend. This was supposed to be such a special night." Tears slid down her cheeks. I gently patted Isabella's shoulder as Carly rolled past on the stretcher.

A light rain began falling, the drops landing on Carly and the rest of us.

Tears from heaven.

Rose and William met us as we loaded Carly into the ambulance, and Meg filled them in on Carly's condition. "I'll call this in to the doc and see if he wants us to intubate now or hold off," Rose said to her partner. "How about you start a line?"

William nodded in agreement and quickly and efficiently placed an intravenous line in Carly's right arm. I noticed that she didn't even flinch when the needle entered her vein.

Rose hung up with the emergency room physician and pulled out an airway kit. "He said to go ahead and intubate, based on her condition," she said. She threaded a flexible plastic tube down Carly's trachea to maintain her airway. "Squeeze the bag valve mask once every five seconds," she instructed Buddy.

When we arrived at the hospital, we wheeled Carly directly into the trauma area and were met by a team of emergency room personnel. It looked as though Carly was about to undergo a rapid assessment and testing.

Will she have to undergo emergency surgery to relieve the pressure on her brain? Are her parents and family on the way here? Will she be okay?

....

A week passed before I got physical therapy orders to evaluate Carly. After reviewing her chart, I checked in with Dana, her ICU nurse. Dana, a passionate RN, was extremely dedicated to her patients. I knew that she would do anything and everything in her power to provide Carly the very best possible care.

"How's she doing?" I asked, almost afraid to hear the answer.

Dana shook her head. "So sad. She hasn't woken up at all yet. The neurologist came by this morning and took her off sedation to do a neuro check, but Carly didn't respond."

My heart sank at the news, but I clung to the realization that sometimes traumatic brain injuries can take an extremely long time to heal. When I entered Carly's room, she looked like she was peacefully sleeping. However, the tracheostomy tube, heart monitor, and intravenous lines told a different story. I noted that someone had carefully braided her long dark hair, which lay neatly next to her on the pillow. I glanced at the bulletin board on the wall and saw a photo of Carly with her arm around Isabella, as well as Carly with a pair of grown-ups, who I assumed were her parents.

She looks so happy and so alive in these photos. A far cry from how she appears now. Why do some people have to pay so dearly for lapses in judgment?

I thought back to the night when we had found Emma Sutton at the bluegrass concert and reflected once again on how incredibly blessed she was to have made a full recovery. I wished the very same for Carly Desimone.

Carly kept her eyes closed and did not respond at all during my evaluation. At the end, I performed range of motion exercises to keep her joints from getting stiff. I hung a copy of how to perform the exercises on the bulletin board next to her photos.

A week later, after Carly weaned off the ventilator, she transferred to a top-notch traumatic brain injury rehabilitation hospital. I prayed that with intense therapy, she might one day heal.

There's always hope.

23

A Leg to Stand On

May the LORD answer you when you are in distress;
may the name of the God of Jacob protect you.
May he send you help from the sanctuary
and grant you support from Zion.

PSALM 20:1-2

What an amazing day!

Fluffy white clouds decorated an azure blue sky. T.J. Fernandez sucked in the clean, crisp air and gave thanks. He almost couldn't believe he was here, riding his brand-new bike in scenic Pine Cove.

One year ago, I wondered if I would ever walk again, let alone ride a bike.

He had peripheral vascular disease as a complication of diabetes. He recalled all those months of leg pain, followed by surgery, and then the rehabilitation. T.J. was not one for self-pity. He was a fighter. Nonetheless, he was glad that it was all behind him. Everything he had gone through was now just a memory of an experience that had helped strengthen his faith and sense of purpose.

Yanked out of his reverie, T.J. was caught completely by surprise when a car suddenly gunned its engine and began accelerating out of a diagonal parking space.

Can't they see me? Don't they know I'm right behind their car? "Stop!" he bellowed. "STOP!"

Although it seemed like super-slow motion to him at the time, it all happened in the span of a few seconds. He was thrown down sideways to the left, his shoulder hitting hard against the pavement.

I can't believe it; they don't hear me. They're going to run over me!

The car slammed on its brakes but too late. T.J. felt the crushing impact and heard a loud crunching noise as the car backed directly over his right leg.

Please, Lord, not my leg! He tried to look down toward his legs, but they were hidden from view beneath the rear of the car. His agonizing shriek filled the morning air, bringing bystanders running from all directions.

The pain is excruciating. He closed his eyes to block some of it out, but it didn't do much good. He could feel his heart pounding uncomfortably in his chest, like a wild bird in a tiny cage. A cold sweat began seeping out of his pores, making him feel oddly hot and cold at the same time.

A panic-stricken young man suddenly appeared at his side. "Sir, I'm so sorry—I didn't see you!" He knelt next to T.J. and placed his right hand on his shoulder.

"It's okay, son. Please, just get me some help. I think my leg is broken." T.J. attempted to keep the anxiety out of his voice. He figured the young fellow felt bad enough already.

"Someone already called for an ambulance, sir. It's on the way," the young man said, obviously frightened and unsure what to do next.

....

DISPATCHER: "Request for first aid in the 1400 block of Kingston Avenue for a bicyclist struck by a car."

Gary grabbed the trauma kit, Mason took the clipboard, and I carried an oxygen bottle as we jumped out of the ambulance and rushed to the accident scene. As we approached, I could see that our patient was an older fellow, maybe in his late sixties or so, wearing a blue-and-gray bike helmet. His glasses lay on the asphalt close to his head. I noticed that one of the lenses was shattered. His legs were hidden beneath the silver car.

"I'm glad you're here," he said. "My name is T.J. Fernandez. It's my right leg. I'm pretty sure it's broken."

As I knelt on the ground at the side of the car to get a better look at T.J.'s legs, I noticed that one of his sneakers lay a few feet from the car. *That's not a good sign if his shoe got ripped clear off his leg.*

"Oh, my goodness," I said softly as I got a better view. The leg wasn't just broken—it was missing from below the knee! Fortunately, T.J. didn't seem to be bleeding much.

"Mason, Gary, can you take a look here for a minute," I said, not wanting to cause T.J. to panic by blurting out that it looked as though half his leg had been literally ripped off!

"How does my leg look?" he asked. "It's okay. You can be honest," he added.

"Where do you feel the pain the most?" Mason asked, evading a direct answer.

"My thigh. I guess you can see from my prosthesis that I have an old, below-the-knee amputation."

I breathed a huge sigh of relief. *So, his leg was missing before the accident.*

"Actually, I don't see your prosthesis," I said. I shimmied farther down to the end of the car and found a crumpled heap of twisted metal and plastic. "Oops, I see it now," I said. "It's just not attached to your leg anymore." That also explained why I initially saw the sneaker a few feet away. It had been ripped off from the prosthesis, not from T.J.'s leg.

"The thigh definitely appears deformed," Gary murmured to Mason and me. "Possible femur fracture."

"Mr. Fernandez, we're going to put a splint on your leg, put a collar around your neck, and put you on a backboard," Mason said.

"Okay, do what you gotta do," T.J. said stoically. "I can take it."

We quickly did an assessment, checked his vital signs, and splinted his thigh. Within a few minutes, we were able to roll him onto a backboard and lift him into the ambulance.

Gary drove the rig, and Mason and I climbed into the back with T.J. "What's your medical history, Mr. Fernandez?" Mason asked, taking hold of a pen and the clipboard.

"Well, let me see," he said, furrowing his brow. "High blood pressure, but I'm on medication for that, so it's under control. I had a heart attack about five years ago. I have peripheral vascular disease too. That's how I lost my right leg in the first place."

"I'm sorry to hear that," I said. "I'm a physical therapist, and I've seen it happen to a lot of people." Therapists treat patients with leg amputations from peripheral vascular disease as well as trauma in both the inpatient and outpatient rehab settings.

"The doctors tried to save it at first. They tried bypass surgery, but that didn't work. Then they sent me for whirlpools with physical therapy when I was in the hospital. But unfortunately, the leg was just too far gone. To be honest with you, the pain got to be so terrible that I started praying that they would just take it off. And as it turned out, after two years of constant pain, when they finally did take it off, it was such a relief."

"It sounds like you did really well after the surgery," I said. "It's impressive that you were out riding a bike."

"Yes. Before the surgery, I was in a wheelchair for close to a year. I worked really hard in rehab, and within six months, I was walking with a cane. I got to be good enough that I didn't even need that after a while. During the past year, my wife and I were able to start going on some of the trips we had always dreamed of. For a while there, I thought we might never be able to go anywhere."

"You're truly a remarkable man," Mason said.

"I'll tell you two young people something. I couldn't have gotten through it all without some help from the Big Man upstairs," he said, pointing to the sky. "And I have a feeling I'll be needing more help from him again real soon. My guess is that I'll be going into surgery either today or tomorrow."

"I work at the hospital," I said. "I'll keep my eye out for you in case you end up needing physical therapy." We routinely receive physical therapy orders to get patients out of bed the very next day after surgery.

"Terrific," he said. "I'm sure I will, and I'll hold you to that. Are we almost there?"

"We're pulling in right now," Mason said. "They'll be able to give you pain meds really soon. Just hang in there for a few more minutes."

"I can do that. Thanks again for everything." He grabbed my hand in his own, and gave it a squeeze. I said a quick silent prayer that everything would go well for Mr. Fernandez and that he would be walking again one day soon.

....

When I entered Mr. Fernandez's room a few days later, his face erupted into a bright smile of recognition. "I knew you'd keep your promise. I'm ready. Let's get out of this bed and into that chair!"

"I love your enthusiasm," I laughed. "Some people cry and moan at the sight of this walker," I said, giving it a little shake.

"No way," T.J. said. "That walker is going to start me on the road to recovery."

"Well, I thought we could try sitting on the edge of the bed first. Then, if you're not too dizzy, Zed and I will help you stand up," I said, gently peeling back his covers.

Zed Nickerson held out his hand and smiled. "Andrea's already told me all about you."

"Andrea helped pick me up off the pavement," T.J. said. "I ended up needing surgery for my femur. But the surgeon assures me that I'm as good as new."

After testing T.J.'s strength and range of motion, I taught him a few simple, beginner exercises for his leg. "Now it's show time," I said, placing my clipboard on the honey oak nightstand. He sat on the edge of the bed with just a small boost from Zed and me.

"You have no idea how good it feels to just sit up again," he said. "This is so exciting. I've been dreaming about this since yesterday."

"Okay," I said. "We'll try standing on the count of three. One, two…" He sprang up onto his left leg before I could even get to three. He stood for about 30 seconds and then took four or five hops with the walker from the bed to the chair. "Fantastic! You're off to a really great start," I said, shaking his hand.

"That's just what I needed today," he said. "Something to build up my morale and self-confidence. I'm leaving for the rehab hospital tomorrow. Now I feel ready."

"Good luck," Zed and I said simultaneously. "You'll do great there."

T.J. was a living testimony to his faith. I knew that his enthusiasm and courage would serve as an inspiration to all the other patients at the rehab hospital.

24

Not Ready to Die

*The LORD looks down from heaven
on all mankind
to see if there are any who understand,
any who seek God.*

PSALM 14:2

Francine Byer spat a wad of blood into her bathroom sink and frowned. *Where in the world is that blood coming from? I need to finish preparing my case for tomorrow.*

Francine was a high-profile criminal-defense attorney. She was extremely good at what she did, partly because she spent a tremendous amount of time doing it. "Cases don't prepare themselves," she was fond of saying to the interns at her law firm.

She grabbed a tissue and wiped the corners of her mouth, removing visible evidence of the blood. She glanced in the bathroom mirror and chose to ignore the yellowness that had crept into her eyes over the past week. *I don't have time to go to a doctor. Whatever that yellowness is, it's just going to have to wait a bit before I can get to my doctor.* Shrugging, she returned to her kitchen table, where all her notes and textbooks were spread out. She knew she was close to a breakthrough, but she would have to push ahead for a few more hours. *Dinner can wait. I'm not up for it anyway, what with spitting up that blood.*

Francine worked quietly for another half hour, pushing off the insistent urge to return to the bathroom and spit out more blood. Finally, worrying that if she didn't go to her sink immediately that the blood might end up on her notes, she gave in. This time, however, the sheer volume of bloody vomit caught her off guard, frightening her.

I better call 911 and have someone check me out. Then, hopefully, I can get back to work.

....

> **DISPATCHER:** "Request for first aid at 684 Chestnut Street for a 62-year-old female vomiting blood."

"Grab the emesis basin, would ya?" Dillon asked as we parked in front of a gray seashore colonial.

A breathtaking Norway spruce graced the front yard, its majestic branches beckoning us toward the front door. *Wow, that tree would look terrific with Christmas lights.* But in contrast to the neighboring homes, 684 Chestnut was devoid of holiday decorations.

Officer Vinnie McGovern met us at the front door. "I'm not sure exactly what's going on," he said. "The patient, Francine Byer, said that she's concerned because she just coughed up some blood. She left it in the bathroom sink if you want to take a look."

Officer McGovern stepped back so we could slip past him. "She said she just wants someone to check her out."

"Sounds like she needs to go to the hospital," I said, pausing to hold the screen door open for Gary.

"That's what I told her, but she didn't want to hear it," Officer McGovern said, shaking his head in disbelief.

We trekked into the kitchen and found Francine sitting at her table. She stood up as we entered the room. "Oh, thanks for coming," she said. "I hate to bother you and bring you all out, but I really just want someone to check my blood pressure."

As Dillon moved closer to Francine, Gary and I backed up and discreetly went down a short hall to peek in the bathroom. My jaw dropped open in shock. This woman was in very serious trouble. With that kind of blood loss, it was frankly astounding that she was still talking and walking around.

"I can't believe how much blood there is," I whispered to Gary.

"Me neither. I'm going to check on where the medics are. The faster we get this lady to the hospital, the better I'll feel," he responded.

I eased my way back into the kitchen just in time to hear Dillon ask when Francine's symptoms started. "When did you notice the yellow in your eyes?" he asked.

Francine waved her hand dismissively. "I guess it's been a week or so. When this case is over, I promise I'll go to a doctor and get that checked out."

"When is your case over?" I asked, figuring she would say in a day or two.

She shrugged. "In a few weeks, I suppose. Sometimes it's hard to know."

"We call that yellow discoloration *jaundice*," Dillon said. "It could mean that you have some sort of problem with your liver. We recommend that you go to the emergency room immediately to stop the bleeding and get thoroughly checked out."

"I really don't want to go to the hospital tonight." Francine frowned. "The timing on this whole thing is not good." She glanced up at the cherry-framed clock hanging above her stove, and her frown deepened.

"Okay, so tell me again," Dillon began patiently. "When was the first time you vomited blood?"

"Well, I've been spitting up blood for the past half hour, though yesterday I did spit out a little bit of blood once in the afternoon. I thought that maybe I had a loose filling or something. It wasn't nearly as much as tonight."

"Any changes in your stools?" I asked. "Have your bowel movements been darker than usual lately, or looked tarry?"

"Well, I'm just not sure. I guess I never look at my stools. Even if they were dark, I probably would have assumed that it was from something I ate," she said.

Just then, Gary reentered the room. "Eight-minute ETA on the medics," he said.

I sat down next to Francine and took her blood pressure while Dillon continued to jot down notes on our call sheet.

"Your blood pressure is 90 over 58. That's low, Francine," I said. "You really need to go to the hospital to get checked out."

"Oh, I don't know. I bet it's always low. How's my pulse?" she asked.

"It's 110, which is on the fast side. And it's a bit weak," I added.

Francine looked indecisive. "You're all recommending that I go to the hospital tonight?" she asked, chewing on her lower lip.

"Yes," Dillon, Gary, Officer McGovern, and I said in unison.

"The sooner the better," Gary added. "You've lost a lot of blood."

"Very well," Francine relented. "But I'd like to pack a few things first. And I need to use the toilet as well." She shoved a few personal items and some papers into a satchel.

Francine disappeared into the restroom and closed the door. I brought our first aid bag back out to the ambulance, and when I returned, she was still in the bathroom. "Francine," Dillon said. "Are you okay in there?"

Just then, I cringed at the sound of more retching. "We have a basin that you can use for that in the ambulance," I called through the door to her. "We should really get moving."

When Francine opened the door, she looked decidedly pale. "Yes, you're definitely right. I need to get to the hospital."

We glanced in and noted that she had vomited copious amounts of bright red blood. It looked like a murder scene! There was blood in the sink, the toilet, and even splashed onto the walls. "Time to go," Gary said, grabbing her under one arm while Dillon supported the other one. We helped her onto our stretcher, which was set up right outside the bathroom door.

Just then, Arthur and Kennisha arrived from the hospital. "Take a peek in the bathroom," I whispered.

As we rolled Francine out the front door, Arthur came up behind us. I could tell from the look on his face that he had indeed checked the bathroom. "We need to really step it up," he said softly, so as not to let Francine hear him. "This is a life-threatening emergency." Then, elevating his voice, he added, "You've lost a lot of blood, and I'm concerned that you might go into shock. I'm going to start an intravenous line as soon as we get into the ambulance to replace some of the fluids you've lost."

"Do you really think that's necessary?" Francine asked. "Maybe the doctor could just give me a blood transfusion or something."

"Yes," Kennisha said for her partner. "We think it's very necessary." I detected a sense of urgency in her voice, and I hoped Francine did as well. She had delayed this trip to the hospital for too long.

Francine appeared subdued in the ambulance. The medics' words seemed to have penetrated her barricade of disbelief. "I'd like to thank you all for your help. I'm not trying to give any of you a hard time," she said. "I guess it's my nature, being an attorney and all. It's just that I'm really busy, and frankly, I just don't have time to get sick."

Kennisha attached a blood pressure cuff to Francine's left arm and pressed the start button on the machine. "I know," she said. "I suppose we all feel like that sometimes. But it's our job to get you to the hospital safely."

I glanced at the blood pressure reading and noted that it had sunk to 84 over 52. *Not good. I'm glad we'll be at the hospital in less than five minutes.*

We lapsed into silence, with Francine obviously deep in her own thoughts. I watched the steady drip, drip, drip of the IV line as it sent fluids into her vein. *I hope that's enough to bring her pressure back up into a safer range.*

We brought Francine straight into a triage room at the hospital, where Dr. Parnell and Maggie, the triage nurse, met us. Realizing that she was in good hands, I stepped out of the room and into the hallway. As I was leaving, I heard Dr. Parnell say, "Esophageal varices."

Esophageal varices are abnormally swollen veins that can start to bleed. A very dangerous condition.

Dillon and Gary rolled our stretcher down the long hallway toward the exit while I trailed a few steps behind. "Oh, I forgot to replace our emesis basin," I said. "I'll be right back." I retraced my steps and noticed with dismay that there was suddenly a flurry of activity in Francine's room.

"Call a code," I heard Maggie say.

My heart filled with sadness for Francine. Just like that, her heart stopped. I knew the medical team would do their best, but I also realized the gravity of Francine's condition. *If only she had made the time to get checked out a week ago or earlier, when she first noticed the yellow eyes. Now it might be too late.*

An hour later, our squad was dispatched for a 57-year-old gentleman with chest pains. As I ran out of the house to grab another oxygen bottle, Arthur and Kennisha's medic rig pulled up to the curb. I looked at them with questioning eyes.

"I know what you're going to ask. I wish I could give you good news, but I can't," Arthur said. "Truth is, I'm pretty shaken up myself still. They pronounced Francine about 20 minutes ago. They never got her pulse back."

"They really tried, but it just wasn't meant to be, I suppose," Kennisha added. "It's really a shame."

"Well, thanks for the update," I said, my heart heavy. Francine Byer hadn't thought she was ready to get sick, let alone die that night. We never truly know when Christ will call us home.

25

Hitting Close to Home

But I, by your great love,
can come into your house;
in reverence I bow down
toward your holy temple.

PSALM 5:7

Mom, how did it go at the doctor's office today?" I asked, twirling the telephone cord around my finger.

"Oh, Andrea, I'm so glad you called! Are you still at work? I was just about to call you," my mom said.

"Yeah, I'm still here, but I'll be leaving in a couple of minutes. Is everything okay?" I thought I detected a note of anxiety in my mother's voice.

"Well, I took Dad to the doctor's office this morning because I felt like his breathing didn't sound quite right to me. The doctor said everything was fine and that his breathing may have sounded like it was a bit off because of his rib fractures."

My dad had broken four ribs a month earlier. They seemed to be healing well, and they hadn't caused him any pain during the past two weeks or so. The fact that they could suddenly be causing such problems was a surprise to me.

"That doesn't make any sense to me, Mom. Why would the rib fractures suddenly affect his breathing?"

"It doesn't make sense to me either. But the doctor said his lungs are clear. I was hoping you could come over here after work and take a listen yourself. I'm really starting to worry." My mom is a class-A worrier, but in this case, she seemed validated.

"I'll be there as soon as I can," I promised. "I'm leaving right now. If you get worried, call for an ambulance. You don't need to wait for me."

"Well, you know your father. He doesn't want to go to the hospital. He said he already went to the doctor and that he didn't find anything wrong with him," Mom said with a sigh.

My dad could be stubborn when it came to the words "emergency room." But at the time, I wasn't too worried. How bad could it be? After all, the doctor had seen him earlier that day and said he was fine.

....

"I'm home," I called out, closing the back door behind me. I headed immediately for the family room, where I knew I would find my dad in his favorite recliner. I wasn't sure what to expect. To my knowledge, my dad had never complained of breathing troubles.

As I anticipated, I found my dad in his chair, with my mom hovering close by. What I didn't anticipate was that he appeared to be in true respiratory distress. He was leaning forward in his chair with his forearms resting on his thighs. His lips were pursed, and the veins on the sides of his neck were distended from the effort to get air in.

I gave them each a quick hug. "Dad, how long have you been breathing like this?" At a glance, I could tell that he definitely belonged in an emergency room.

"Well, it's been gradually getting worse all day," he puffed.

I grabbed my stethoscope and placed it over his lungs, carefully listening to his breath sounds. I could clearly hear abnormal sounds each time he breathed in, and his lung sounds were diminished at the bases. I felt a wave of apprehension sweep over me, the first icy fingers of fear taking root in my core.

"We need to go to the hospital right now," I said firmly. "No ifs, ands, or buts."

What happened next scared me even more. My dad simply said okay.

He must feel truly terrible if he's agreeing to go to the hospital without any argument. I grabbed the cordless phone off the end table and dialed our local police department. *Okay, Andrea, stay calm. Don't let Dad hear the fear in your voice.*

"Pine Cove Police Department," Dispatcher Franklin said.

"Hi, it's Andrea from the first aid squad," I said, willing my voice not to shake. "I need an ambulance at our house. My dad's having difficulty breathing." I quickly rattled off our address.

"Okay, I'll send an ambulance right away," Dispatcher Franklin promised. "Please stay on the line until the police officers arrive at your home." I handed the phone to my mom and turned back to my father, so I could check his blood pressure and pulse. I noticed that his skin was moist, probably from the effort he was exerting just to breathe.

Within a couple minutes, the doorbell rang. Officer Endicott stepped inside. "Hi," he said, handing me an oxygen tank and mask. "I just heard that the paramedics aren't available." I tried not to let my anxiety tick one notch higher from this news. I knew that my dad needed the medics, but it seemed we were going to have to do without. I'd just have to let the triage nurse know what was going on as soon as we arrived at the hospital. I placed high-flow oxygen on him, fervently hoping it would help his breathing.

Helen and Meg knocked and stepped inside. I don't recall ever being so glad to see them both. "I brought the first aid bag in, but I guess you probably took a blood pressure already and everything. How's your dad doing?" Helen asked.

"Not so good, I'm afraid. And there are no medics available. I think we better get a move on. Thank you both so much for getting here so fast."

"Of course," Meg said. "That's what friends are for. I'm going to grab the stretcher and we'll get rolling."

Dad lifted his hand to wave hello, but didn't say anything. I knew he was trying to save his breath; the effort to speak would have been too much.

"Dad, we're going to help you stand up and get on the stretcher," I said, as I stood by his side. Helen and I gave him a boost up and helped him take a few steps to the stretcher.

"I'm driving," Helen said to my mom. "Why don't you ride up front with me?"

"Thank you," my mom replied. "I want to stay close to him, and I don't trust myself to drive right now."

A minute later, we were on the way to Bakersville Hospital. My gut clenched as I could plainly see my father's condition was deteriorating. Fast. Right before my eyes.

"Helen," I called up to the front of the ambulance. "Can you please call ahead to the emergency room? Tell them we're coming in."

"Got it," she said, and I felt the rig go a little bit faster.

"His pulse ox is low despite the oxygen," Meg whispered. She was clearly worried.

The ride to the hospital passed by slowly, each agonizing second seeming to last an eternity. At last, I glanced out the window and realized with relief that we were only about five blocks from the hospital.

"Andrea, I have a bit of a problem," Helen called back to us. "I've hit upon some sort of detour. I'm going to try to figure it out."

I wanted to shout, "No! Please, no detour!" But instead, I managed to say in a strained voice, "Okay, but we need to get there really fast."

I watched my father's breathing closely. It seemed to be getting more rapid and shallow. *Should we start assisting his breathing with a bag valve mask? Lord, please guide me and make sure I do the right thing.*

"Okay, we're back on track, thank goodness," Helen said. "We'll be there in a minute."

Meg changed the oxygen from our main tank to our portable unit, and I squeezed my dad's hand tightly, wishing I never had to let go. He looked into my eyes, and we both acknowledged without words exactly how critical his situation had become.

We rushed Dad down the long corridor toward the emergency room. Maggie met us in the lobby. Taking one glance at my father, she said, "Room 2—now."

I glanced toward Room 2, and I saw with relief that one of my best friends from childhood, Penny, was standing there. "Andrea, right this way. I'm going to be his nurse," she said.

I gave Penny a quick hug. "I'm really scared," I whispered to her. I had the utmost confidence in Penny's ability. I trusted her with my father's life.

Meg, Helen, and I lifted my dad from our stretcher to the one in Room 2.

"Dr. Parnell is on tonight," Penny said, briefly peeking outside the curtain and down the hall to see if she could spot her. "I'm going to get her right now." True to her word, she returned less than ten seconds later with Dr. Parnell in tow.

"CPAP, right?" Penny asked.

"Yes," Dr. Parnell replied. "And get respiratory here, stat." Everything happened quickly after that. The room buzzed with activity. Soon an abundance of lines and tubes were sticking out of my dad. They placed him on a CPAP machine, which seemed to give him some relief. A CPAP (continuous positive airway pressure) machine uses air pressure to help keep a person's airways open.

Shortly after we arrived, my sister Marie joined Mom and me in the hallway while the emergency room staff attended to Dad. My mom gripped my sister's and my hands tightly, and we squeezed hers back. I knew that our faith and our mutual love for my dad and for each other would help us through this nightmare.

A little while later, Penny stepped into the hallway. "Good news," she said. "He's stable, and we're sending him up to the intensive care unit right now." Dr. Parnell explained that my father had developed congestive heart failure. He spent several days recuperating in the hospital before being discharged home.

Thank you, Lord, for letting my father live. And thank you for the precious gift of my friend Penny and all the staff and first aid members who helped us that day.

26

Impressing Your Date

My shield is God Most High,
who saves the upright in heart.

PSALM 7:10

C hip Hughes sped along Jefferson Avenue on his new mountain bike, deep in thought. The fragrant smell of freshly cut grass, the vibrant burst of color from tulips and cherry blossom trees, and the cacophony of sounds from hungry seagulls were all lost on him. All Chip could think about was that he was going on a first date tonight with the girl of his dreams, Melanie.

After months of trying to muster the courage, he had finally called Melanie a few days ago. To his surprise, the conversation went great, and the next thing he knew, he had a dinner date set up.

What should I wear? Jeans or khakis? Where should I take her? Casual or someplace more fancy? What if I run out of things to talk about? If dinner goes well, what should we do afterward? Ice cream and a walk on the boardwalk? Chip had recently turned 19, and he didn't have much experience dating.

Chip didn't see the car until it was too late. He was thrust violently out of his pleasant reverie when the front tire of his bike struck hard against the rear fender of a green sedan, which was parallel parked close to the curb. His bike stopped abruptly, but he felt his body become airborne as he sailed over the handlebars. The flying sensation didn't last long, however. His body exploded in pain as he burst headfirst through the car's rear window.

....

"Heel, Mittens, heel," Ginny Jacobson instructed her golden retriever puppy as she approached her car. The pair had just enjoyed a pleasant walk around Weeping Willow Lake. Training Mittens was turning out to be more work than Ginny expected, but she was enjoying it. Ginny paused, puzzled at first, and then exasperated. "Honestly, Mittens, I don't understand people today. Who would just abandon their bike in the road like that? For goodness' sake, if I had approached my car from the other direction, I wouldn't have even seen it. I would have backed up and run right over it. It would have wrecked the bike, and probably would have messed up my car too." Mittens cocked his head and barked once as if in agreement.

"Oh, my goodness! I don't believe it—someone broke my window! I was so focused on the bike, I didn't even notice at first." Tugging on Mittens's leash, she pulled him closer to the car to get a better view. "Hard to see much with these tinted windows," she muttered. At that precise moment, the hair on the back of Ginny's neck stood up.

What in the world is that noise? That creepy, horrible noise! It sounds like the way people breathe in those horror movies. Reaching into her pocket, she grabbed her remote to unlock the car, and taking a deep breath, she wrenched the back door open.

A cool, bloody hand flopped out the door and brushed against Ginny's calf. Almost before she realized what she was staring at, a bloodcurdling scream burst forth from her lips. A young man was sprawled out across her rear seat, blood dripping from his hands and face.

Is he alive? Dear Lord, please tell me this person is alive.

....

DISPATCHER: "Request for first aid on the 300 block of Jefferson Avenue for a cyclist versus a car. The patient is currently unconscious and unresponsive."

"He's out cold," Colleen said, taking hold of Chip's head to stabilize it in case he had a neck injury. "Chip, open your eyes for me," she commanded. Chip kept his eyes closed, though he began to make groaning noises.

Alec opened the rear door on the other side and squeezed himself in along the floorboard. "Wake up," he said, gently rubbing on Chip's breastbone. At the time, it was common to use a technique called a sternal rub to help determine a patient's level of consciousness. If a person reacts to the chest rub, he is "responsive to painful stimuli." Chip groaned louder in response to the rub, indicating he could feel pain.

That's a good sign. It's certainly better than no response at all.

Alec did a head-to-toe assessment and checked Chip's blood pressure and pulse. Just as he was finishing, Chip's eyes snapped open. For a few seconds he was silent, his mind trying to figure out exactly where he was and why we were staring at him. "Where am I?" he asked.

"You seem to have had an accident with your bike," Colleen said. "We're going to take you to the hospital to get checked out," she said reassuringly.

Chip nodded his head, answered some questions for Colleen, and then lapsed into silence. I slid a cervical collar around his neck, and then we maneuvered him onto a backboard. As we were sliding him out of the car onto the stretcher, Chip asked, "What day is it?"

"Saturday," Alec replied. "A little after two o'clock."

"That's what I was afraid you were going to say. Do you think they're going to admit me? I have my first date with someone tonight."

I truly wasn't sure if Chip would get admitted or not. It was certainly a possibility, given his mechanism of injury and the fact that he was unconscious for a few minutes. At a minimum, he would be diagnosed with a concussion. He'd need further tests to see if anything else was wrong. As I gazed at his torn lip and the lacerations on his forehead and chin, I figured that he would probably be getting a bunch of stitches.

Well, if Chip somehow manages to go on his date tonight, he sure is going to have lots of interesting talking points regarding why his face looks the way it does.

Of course, abrasions and lacerations heal. Chip was truly blessed that he was wearing a bicycle helmet, or the outcome of his accident could have been much worse.

27

Free at Last

*The Lord is the Spirit, and where the Spirit
of the Lord is, there is freedom.*

2 CORINTHIANS 3:17

slowly pedaled along on my beach patrol mountain bike, enjoying the gentle sea breeze on my face and arms. It was about 11 o'clock on a weekday morning. So far, my shift had been pleasantly calm and quiet. As my gaze swept across the sparkling blue ocean and clean sandy beaches, I thanked God for the gift of such an incredibly beautiful day.

A flicker of something out of the ordinary caught my attention on the far side of the boardwalk, close to the dunes. I brought my bike to a halt and slowly walked over to the railing. As I peered over the edge, I noticed a middle-aged man lying on his stomach in the sand, with his legs under the boardwalk and his torso in the sun. He had on a pair of blue jeans, and his shirt was folded under his cheek to act as a pillow. One of his arms and half of his back were sunburned the brightest shade of red I had ever witnessed. In sharp contrast, the other arm and the rest of his back were the pastiest shade of white I had ever seen, as if his skin hadn't seen the sun for quite a few years.

I wonder what this man's story is. Is he unconscious? Injured? Ill? Or just sleeping off a bad hangover? I hesitated for several minutes, watching him closely to see if he showed any sort of movement.

An older man wearing a plaid bathing suit and a blue baseball cap wandered over to me. "He's been lying there since I got here at nine. He hasn't moved a bit in the last two hours," he said.

"Thanks," I replied. "I think I'll see if he's okay." I didn't want to bother the man if he was just trying to enjoy a relaxing day at the beach, but something didn't seem right. For starters, he was lying on the west side of the boardwalk, farthest from the ocean. In addition, if he didn't get out of the sun soon, he was heading toward a terrible case of sun poisoning.

Mustering my courage, I slid between the two boardwalk rails and jumped gently down onto the beach. I hoped my landing might jar the man awake, but no such luck. I squatted near him and studied him more intently. His jeans appeared old and worn, with a large hole visible in the seat of his pants. The part of his T-shirt that I could see sticking out from under his head appeared equally worn and faded. I noticed that he was still wearing his socks, though his sneakers lay close by on the sand.

Wearing socks on the beach? Another red flag...

I leaned forward and gently tapped his shoulder. No response. I tapped a little bit harder. Still no response. "Sir," I said softly. No reply. "Sir," I said more loudly and tapped his shoulder harder.

The man stirred, blinked several times, and then lifted his head to look at me. His bland look of confusion turned to one of dismay when he realized I was wearing a police uniform. "Am I under arrest?" he asked.

"No, no. I was just worried about you. Your skin is so red, you look like you're turning into a lobster," I said. "I just wanted to make sure you're okay."

The man sat up, looked at his crimson arm, and winced. "That's going to hurt," he murmured with a sigh.

"What's your name, sir?" I asked. "Do you live around here?" I wanted to see how he answered the questions to determine if he was coherent.

"My name is Slade," he replied, sliding himself into the shade of the boardwalk.

"Where do you live?" I prompted, noting that he had skirted the question.

"Well, the truth is, I just got out of prison yesterday. My wife divorced me while I was away, so I really don't have a place to go," he said, carefully avoiding eye contact by staring down at the sand.

Free at last and nowhere to go. Homeless. How incredibly sad.

"Do you have a friend you could stay with until you get back on your feet?"

"I've been thinking about that. Where am I right now?" he asked, gazing around.

"Pine Cove," I replied.

"Oh. Well, maybe I could walk to the train station," Slade said. "I do have a friend who lives a half hour north of here. I think he would let me crash for a while. The problem is that I don't think I have enough money for the train fare."

"Well, if you'll give me a minute, I'll radio our dispatcher to send a patrolman here to help."

Slade frowned. "I don't know if that's such a good idea. How can you be sure that he's not going to arrest me? I don't want to go right back where I came from. I can't. It'll kill me if I have to go back there."

"He's not going to arrest you, I promise," I said persuasively. Without waiting any longer, I radioed headquarters. Soon Officer Endicott joined us under the boardwalk, and I explained Slade's dilemma.

"Did you walk here straight from the train station?" Officer Endicott asked.

"More or less, with a few detours," Slade replied. "To be honest with you, I'm a bit fuzzy on the details."

"Well, let's call your friend so he knows to expect you. Then I'll drive you to the train station, and I'll pay for your fare to meet him."

A look of profound relief and gratitude flooded Slade's face. "Thank you," he said simply. With that, he slipped his sneakers on, pulled his T-shirt over his head, and rose to his feet. He nodded to me and then ambled away with Officer Endicott.

I felt saddened that Slade's first day out of prison was off to a rocky start, but at the same time, I was hopeful that he was now on the right track toward being able to truly enjoy his newfound freedom.

Dear Lord, please take Slade into your loving embrace and lead him on the path toward peace and redemption.

28

Letting Go

The cords of death entangled me;
the torrents of destruction overwhelmed me.
The cords of the grave coiled around me;
the snares of death confronted me.
In my distress, I called to the LORD;
I cried to my God for help.
From his temple he heard my voice;
my cry came before him, into his ears.

PSALM 18:4-6

It wasn't supposed to happen this quickly. I thought I had more time. I'm not ready yet. Please, Lord. Not yet. Not like this. I want my family to be with me.

With trembling fingers, Autumn Dean turned up the knob on her oxygen machine as high as it would go, but it simply wasn't high enough.

I can't get any air in. It's getting so hard to breathe. I need more oxygen. What should I do?

Autumn had been diagnosed with cancer three years ago to the day. She fought hard, undergoing surgery and then chemotherapy. Just when she thought that it was all over and that she could finally move on with her life, the insidious cancer returned. She had to undergo more painful surgery and another round of chemotherapy. And finally, one month before this day, came the crushing words from her oncologist: "I'm so very sorry, Autumn. At this point, we've done everything that we can. I think we need to talk about going on hospice."

Hospice. It was still very difficult for Autumn to grasp that the end of her life on earth was near, that the long fight was over, that it was time to start thinking about letting go. Nevertheless, a few short days later, the horrible hospital bed appeared in her living room. How she hated looking at that bed and all that it represented: the finality of it all. In fact, she fervently wished she didn't have to spend another minute in that bed. Unfortunately, she was too weak to climb the stairs to make it to her own room on the second floor. And so, the bed stayed. Autumn sat down on the edge of the dreaded bed and tried to catch her breath.

I can't go on much longer like this.

She closed her eyes for a minute and then opened them and let her gaze sweep across the room—the China cabinet with her antique porcelain teddy bear collection, the beloved colorful quilt that her mother had made for her so many years ago, and the statue of Saint Michael, which her husband had received as a confirmation gift when he was just a boy. Grief, sharp in its bitter intensity, pierced her soul.

I will miss my life here so much. Please be with me, Lord, and when the time comes, help me to move on in peace.

Autumn's daughter, Rachel, had spent the past week here with her. The time together had been bittersweet for both as they reminisced together. Rachel had loaded her wheelchair in the car trunk and taken her down to the boardwalk for some fresh air and a glimpse of the ocean. The visit rejuvenated Autumn's sagging spirits. She wished the visit could last forever, but her daughter had left the day before to check on her family and collect a few more belongings. She promised she would be back by this weekend.

I'm sorry, Rachel. I'm not sure I'm going to make it that long.

As tears of uncertainty trickled down Autumn's cheeks, she grabbed a tissue off the end table in a halfhearted attempt to wipe them away.

Call the hospice nurse. Remember, she gave you her card. It's got to be around here somewhere. She'll know what to do. She should be able to help.

Digging through a pile of magazines, Autumn found the elusive card. With trembling fingers, she grabbed her cordless phone. Hesitating for just a second, she dialed the number.

When Autumn hung up the telephone a few minutes later, she was filled with unease.

Fifteen to thirty minutes until she can get here? How am I going to make it that long?

The receptionist who answered the phone had told her to sit tight, and a nurse would be there soon to help her. But suddenly, 15 minutes seemed like an eternity. Autumn knew what she wanted to do.

Forget about hospice and the DNR. I need help now.

....

DISPATCHER: "Request for first aid at 400 Horizon Avenue for a cancer patient with difficulty breathing."

"Oh no!" my mom exclaimed, hearing my pager. "That's Autumn's house." My mom and Autumn had been friends for as long as I could remember. Mom had been upset four weeks earlier when Autumn broke the sad news to her that she was going on hospice. My mom didn't like to talk about it much, but I knew that she would miss her friend terribly. She'd visited Autumn two weeks before and had taken her some homemade chicken noodle soup.

"Food for the soul," Autumn had said to her.

"You better hurry," Mom said anxiously. "Please call me if you need me to come over and help. I'll stay right here by the phone."

Since Autumn lived close by, I jogged straight there and rang the front doorbell. "Come in," she said weakly.

Autumn looked extremely gaunt and feeble. I rushed to her side and gave her a quick, gentle hug. "What's going on?" I asked. "Is it your breathing?"

Autumn nodded, her light blue eyes huge in her pale face. "It happened so fast. I was okay earlier today, but then, *wham*! I tried turning up my oxygen, but it's not enough."

"I'll give you an oxygen mask as soon as the police department gets here," I said. "That'll give you more oxygen than the nasal tube does."

Autumn grabbed my hand and squeezed it tightly. "I'm so glad you came. I don't want to be alone. It's so comforting to see a familiar face."

I squeezed her dear, sweet, loving hand back. "I'm so sorry you're going through this," I said, but the words sounded inadequate to my ears.

"I wasn't supposed to call you, you know. The nurse said not to call 911, but I did anyway," Autumn said, a frown creasing her brow.

"Why not?" I asked. "I mean, if you're having trouble breathing..."

"Well, your mom probably told you that I'm on hospice," Autumn replied. "And I have a DNR."

DNR stands for "do not resuscitate." If a person has a DNR, we don't perform CPR.

"Don't ever feel like you can't call us," I said. "You have to do what feels right. Follow your gut," I said, picking up a handmade quilt from a chair on the other side of the room and carefully draping it over Autumn's shoulders.

"I didn't think it would end like this," she whispered. "I thought it would be more peaceful. And I want Rachel to be with me," she said, pulling the edges of the quilt more tightly around her shoulders.

"We'll get Rachel," I said. "She can be back here within a few hours."

"Please have someone call her. Tell her that I need her to come back right away. I don't think there's much time." Autumn glanced at the digital clock on her end table and then looked away. "I feel ready spiritually but not emotionally. I know the Lord is going to take me home, but I just need a little more time."

"I understand. And it seems like it's all happening so quickly," I said, sliding my fingers to her radial artery so I could check her pulse. She was working very hard just to breathe.

Thank goodness the police will be here any second. She needs high-flow oxygen right away.

"I don't want to die in this house. I can't bear it. I thought I wanted to, but I've changed my mind," she said, a pleading look haunting her eyes. "I hope the nurse understands."

The doorbell chimed, and Officer Sims stepped inside. "Hi, Mrs. Dean. I'm sorry you're not feeling well today." Noting her respiratory distress, he pulled a non-rebreather mask out of his first aid kit and handed it to me. "Do you want 15 liters?"

I nodded in reply as I placed the mask on Autumn's face and then tightened the straps to ensure a snug fit. "Take nice deep breaths, in through your nose and out through your mouth."

"Yes, I can feel the oxygen now. Thank you so much, both of you. Thank God you came. I could never have lasted until the nurse arrived."

A moment later, Helen and Gary arrived with the ambulance. I quickly filled out the call sheet while Helen took Autumn's blood pressure and respiratory rate. Officer Sims and Gary brought in the stretcher. Just as we were about to help Autumn onto it, the hospice nurse arrived.

"Hello, I'm Nancy, the nurse from hospice," she said briskly. Seeing our stretcher, she said, "I think there's been some sort of mistake. Why are these people here, Autumn?"

"I panicked. I couldn't breathe," Autumn said, her eyes downcast.

"I thought you understood that we have a plan for this," Nancy said firmly. "The ambulance should never have been called."

"But I want to go to the hospital," she replied softly.

"You have a DNR. You're on hospice. I can give you morphine to make your breathing more comfortable," Nancy said, softening her voice. "Just like we've talked about over the past few weeks."

"If she wants to go to the hospital, then I think she has a right to change her mind," I said, trying to keep the defensive edge out of my voice.

A look of gratitude and relief flashed across Autumn's face. And in that instant, I knew the right thing to do.

Forget the stupid DNR. I don't care if Autumn is on hospice. She needs to go to the hospital, where she'll be more comfortable.

"This is highly unusual," Nancy said. "The hospice plan is in place for a reason. When a person is on hospice, emergency squads really should not get involved."

"Yes, I understand all that," Autumn said. "But I'm still glad I called them." Her eyes brightened with sudden determination.

"Do you understand that you may need to revoke your hospice benefits if you go to the hospital?" Nancy asked.

"I know that you're just doing your job. Frankly, I don't care about my hospice benefits. I just want to go to the hospital. But thank you kindly for coming out for me," Autumn said, her voice growing stronger. Turning away from Nancy and toward us, she said, "I'm ready to go now."

....

Autumn closed her eyes, but sleep eluded her. When she opened her eyes again, she was surrounded by Rachel and her entire family. She glanced down and noticed her dear family quilt was lying across her bed.

Rachel stood up and gave her mom a hug and kiss. "We stopped at the house on the way," she explained. "I thought you might like to have the quilt here."

"You always know just what to do," Autumn said. A look of peace settled across her face, replacing the fear and worry from earlier. "I'm so glad you're all here with me. I love you all more than words can describe."

"We love you too, Mom," Rachel said, her voice tight with emotion. "Always."

"I'm so very tired. Now that you're here, I can finally get some rest." She closed her eyes, but her fingers remained clasped around Rachel's. Six hours later, as the sun rose over the Atlantic with its rays sparkling like diamonds upon the water, Autumn Dean went to her new home with the Lord.

29

You Scream, I Scream!

*He will yet fill your mouth with laughter
and your lips with shouts of joy.*

JOB 8:21

rozen yogurt," Gary said, briefly taking off his baseball cap and running his fingers through his hair. "I'm so hot! We need frozen yogurt."

"I'm in," I said without hesitation. "I'm starving." It had been a busy afternoon. A little after lunch, our squad transported a middle-aged woman with a history of asthma who was complaining of difficulty breathing to the emergency room. Her shortness of breath had been gradually increasing over several days, and the oppressive July air wasn't helping.

As soon as we had returned to our first aid building, we had received another call to the other side of town for an elderly man with chest pain and shortness of breath. He surmised that he had overdone it by pulling weeds from his front garden bed in the hot summer sun.

Now we found ourselves once more at our first aid building. This time, Gary and I were both in the mood for an ice-cold treat.

We decided to order the frozen yogurt to go and eat it back at the squad building. A mere 15 minutes later, we were back on the road heading east to headquarters, with two large cups of vanilla-chocolate swirl. I had mini chocolate chips on mine, and Gary chose crushed peanut butter cups as his topping. Gary was driving, so I peeled up the plastic cover on my yogurt and took a few test bites.

I glanced up from my frozen yogurt bliss when Gary exclaimed, "Look at that car—it stopped at the intersection, but now it's starting to go!" I watched with dismay as an older-model brown sedan slowly rolled past a stop sign and headed directly into the middle of the intersection. We both watched in mesmerized horror as the sedan continued its slow-motion journey. A teal-green minivan was heading west toward the intersection, and it was too close to stop in time. The minivan smashed into the sedan, lost control, and began careening wildly down the road—directly toward us!

I heard the sound of squealing tires coupled with a muffled scream. I braced myself. "Hang on!" Gary yelled, tightening his grip on the steering wheel while pushing down hard on the brakes.

I closed my eyes and waited for the inevitable crash. By the grace of God, it didn't happen. Instead, the minivan swerved away from us at the last possible second and went up an embankment, finally coming to rest against a birch tree.

Gary grabbed his portable officer's radio and spoke directly to police headquarters. "We need the police and first aid for a two-car motor vehicle accident," he said, adding our location.

We jumped out of Gary's car and rushed to the minivan. A middle-aged woman and a girl who looked to be her teenage daughter sat in the front seats, a look of shock on their faces. The first thing I noticed was the copious amount of blood. It was on the steering wheel, splashed onto the front windshield, and virtually covering the two women. It stood in sharp contrast to their pastel-colored T-shirts, oozing downward in ominous dark streaks.

"Hi, I'm Gary, and this is Andrea. We're with the Pine Cove First Aid Squad. How are you doing? The police and an ambulance are on the way." He eased open the driver's side door so we could better access the patients.

"We're shaken up, but I think we're basically okay," the woman replied, glancing over at her daughter and patting her forearm. "I just couldn't believe the way that car came out in front of us like that. There was no way to stop in time or swerve around it."

"You've lost a lot of blood," I said, peering into the car while slipping on a pair of gloves I happened to have in my pocket. With that amount of blood, I figured they must have some serious lacerations.

"What blood?" the woman asked, perplexed, glancing around. "Am I bleeding?" She turned to her daughter. "Margot, are you sure you're okay? Did you get hurt? Are you bleeding?"

Margot let out a giggle. "Mom, I think that's our ice cream." She ran her finger across the glove compartment and placed her fingertip in her mouth. "Yep, it's our chocolate ice cream all right."

I had been so sure that it was blood that it took a second for my brain to register that it truly was just a sweet, icy-cold treat. Apparently, the pair had also found a grab-and-go midafternoon snack.

Within a few short minutes, the police and our first aid squad arrived. Fortunately, the person driving the sedan was also uninjured. Gary and I returned to his car and hurried to gobble down what was left of our melting frozen-yogurt treats.

30

The Miracle of Bethany Walker

You, LORD, are a shield around me,
my glory, the One who lifts my head high.
I call out to the LORD,
and he answers me from his holy mountain.

PSALM 3:3-4

Bethany Walker's eyes popped open, and she rolled to her side to look at her alarm clock. A moonbeam crept through a slat in her window blinds, casting a narrow ray of light across her bedroom floor.

Oh no, half past midnight. I know it'll be tough to fall back asleep.

Bethany knew from experience that whenever she happened to awaken in the early morning hours, she usually had difficulty going back to sleep. Invariably, her mind would start racing, thinking about one thing and then another. Before she knew it, she would be wide awake, tossing and turning and wishing desperately that she was back asleep again.

Bethany gradually became aware of a dull ache along the left side of her jaw. *What did I eat today? I wonder if my old TMJ problem is acting up. Well, now that I'm awake, I might as well go to the kitchen and get a drink of water. Maybe that'll help me to fall back asleep again.*

With a sigh of resignation, she swung her feet off the bed and sat on the edge of her mattress. She rubbed the side of her jaw and hoped that the soreness would fade away quickly.

Slowly, Bethany stood up and glanced across the bed toward her

212 On Heaven's Doorstep

husband, Alan, who was still sleeping soundly. Careful not to awaken him, she treaded softly across the carpet and out into the hallway, closing the door behind her.

That's funny. I'm starting to feel a bit lightheaded. I better get that glass of water.

Touching her hand along the wall to steady herself, she headed down the hallway toward the kitchen.

....

It was half past midnight on a cool autumn night in late September. I shivered as the chilly breeze cut straight through me. My sweatshirt had felt just right earlier in the day, but now it didn't provide enough warmth. As much as I wanted to hold on to summer, I knew it was time to accept that it was truly over.

"Grab on to that side of the cot and we'll lift her in," Jessie said, interrupting my thoughts. About 15 minutes earlier, our squad had been dispatched for an elderly woman who'd fallen and injured her left shoulder. We had put a sling and cold pack on her shoulder, and now we were about to transport her to Bakersville Hospital. Together, we lifted the stretcher into the ambulance. As I let go of the stretcher, our pagers went off again.

DISPATCHER: "Request for first aid at 524 Shady Grove Lane for an unresponsive person."

"Jose, Andrea, and I will go. You guys take this one," Jessie said to Helen and several of our other members. "Jose has his car here. He can drive us back to the building and we can get another rig."

"Sounds good," Helen said. "I'll radio to dispatch that we're sending three members back to the building to pick up an ambulance for the second call."

Jose, Jessie, and I climbed into Jose's sedan. "That address sounds familiar, but I can't quite place it," I said, searching my memory.

"I'm pretty sure it's the Walkers' house," Jessie replied. "We were there last year for Mr. Walker when he got dizzy in his bedroom and fell."

"That sounds about right. I remember that call," I agreed. I'd known Bethany and Alan Walker and their children for many years, but I hadn't realized that Alan's father lived with them until we received a first aid call for him. Their son, Cole, was a couple years ahead of me in school. Bethany Walker was known for being a kind and thoughtful person, and my parents spoke very highly of her and her husband.

"Yes, it's definitely the Walkers'," Jose chimed in. "I just passed by there the other day." Jose pulled up and parked by our first aid building, and the three of us jumped out of his car and into an ambulance. "Responding to Shady Grove Lane," he said to the dispatcher, steering the rig out of the parking lot and heading with lights and sirens in the direction of the first aid call.

"Be advised as per officers on the scene that CPR is now in progress," the dispatcher replied. "Expedite."

"Not good," Jessie muttered. "Grab the defibrillator and the suction. I'll get the kit and call sheet."

"Got it," I replied. I assumed that the call was for Alan's father.

Jose had barely brought the rig to a halt when Jessie and I jumped out of the back of the ambulance. Alan Walker stood on the brick sidewalk with Cole, close to the entrance of their home.

"Andrea, Jessie, quick! Do something!" he exclaimed. The urgency and sheer desperation in his voice affected me deeply.

Dear Lord, he's counting on us to help his father. Please be with us. I don't want to let him down.

Jessie threw open the screen door, and we passed through a dimly lit living room into a bright kitchen. Sergeant Flint and Officer McGovern were performing CPR on a person who lay on the floor, close to the kitchen's island. I glanced at the patient's face, and my heart quickened in horror when I realized it was not the elder Mr. Walker at all. It was his daughter-in-law, Bethany!

No wonder Alan is so distraught. It's his wife who's not breathing and doesn't have a pulse!

Bethany lay on her back on the tile floor, her nightgown already cut away by the police to expose her chest for compressions.

"We tried to shock once, but no shock was advised," Sergeant Flint said. "Why don't you take over? I think the defibrillator is going to reanalyze in about 30 seconds."

I knelt next to Bethany's head and helped with the ventilations. At that moment, Jose entered the kitchen. "Oh, no, not Bethany," he said, shaking his head in disbelief. We had all been so certain that the call would be for Bethany's father-in-law.

"Press to analyze," the defibrillator said.

"I've got it," Jessie said. "Everyone clear," he added, waving his arm over Bethany's body to make sure none of us was touching her.

Dear Lord, we need your help right now. Bethany Walker is way too young to die. Please let the shock work!

The pressure was on. The stakes were high. A woman's life hung in the balance, and her family was counting on us. Beads of sweat broke out on my forehead. I held my breath as Jessie pressed the shock button.

"Check for a pulse," he said. I glanced at Jessie's face. I could tell this call was affecting him as much as me. None of us wanted to let the Walkers down.

I placed my fingers on Bethany's carotid artery, hoping against hope. "No pulse," I said with disappointment. "Continue CPR."

Officer McGovern took over chest compressions. Jose went to speak to the family and find out what events had transpired prior to Bethany's collapse. "Three-minute ETA on the medics," Sergeant Flint said.

Hang in there, Mrs. Walker. This isn't over yet. We'll keep trying. Your family loves you and needs you.

"Time to analyze again," Jessie said, once more waving his arm over Bethany's body to make sure we weren't touching her. "Everybody clear." Gingerly, he pressed the shock button. "Check for a pulse."

Dear Lord, please let it work this time.

I felt Bethany's carotid pulse. "I think I feel something," I said. "It's faint, but I definitely think I feel a pulse." My spirit started to fill with hope.

Come on, Mrs. Walker. We're all rooting for you!

I adjusted my fingers and felt again. "There's a strong carotid now," I said. "Hold chest compressions."

At that moment, Alan peered through the entrance into the kitchen. In his eyes, I saw a jumble of hope and fear. "How's she doing?" he asked.

"We're doing everything possible," Sergeant Flint replied. "The paramedics will be here momentarily from the hospital. They'll start an IV line and put a tube down her throat to help her breathe."

Just then, paramedics Ty and Paula stepped through the front door. Jessie quickly filled them in. "After the third shock, her heart started beating again," he finished.

Paula knelt by Bethany's head. "Her pupils are dilated and nonreactive," she said to Ty. I knew this was not a good sign; pupils that are fixed and dilated can indicate a poor prognosis. Carefully, Paula intubated Bethany to control her airway.

Ty checked her lung sounds while I squeezed the bag valve mask. "Tube placement is good," he said. "Let's get moving."

As a team, we rolled Bethany onto a backboard and lifted her onto our stretcher. Although her pulse had returned, she remained unconscious and completely unresponsive. Her right arm started to slide down off the stretcher. Carefully, I lifted it back up and tightened the cot's upper seatbelt to hold her arm securely against her body.

"May I ride to the hospital in the ambulance with you?" Alan asked, squeezing my shoulder. "I want to stay close to Bethany, and I really don't feel up to driving."

"Of course," I said. I took his arm and led him to the front seat of the ambulance. The pallor of his face stood in sharp contrast to his dark navy T-shirt.

"I'll drive and meet you up there, Dad," Cole said. I could tell he was struggling to hold it together for his father's sake.

Jessie and I climbed into the back of the rig to continue working with Bethany. "We're taking you to the hospital. They'll be able to help you there," I said, hoping that on some level, Bethany would be able to hear my words.

You've come this far, Mrs. Walker. Please, please just try to hang in there.

Jessie took over breathing for Bethany with the bag valve mask while I worked on getting a blood pressure. "It's 110 over 70," I said, jotting it down on our call sheet. Meanwhile, Paula continued injecting various cardiac medications through the IV. Out of the corner of my eye, I could see Alan turning around in his chair in the front seat of the ambulance, trying to see how his wife was doing.

Heavy hearted but still hopeful, we dropped off Bethany at the emergency room. I knew that whatever happened, her family would have a difficult road ahead.

....

Five long days passed. "I heard Mrs. Walker is still completely unresponsive. I ran into her husband at the hospital yesterday. Alan said the doctors seem to think there's very little hope for recovery. He said one of the doctors told him to start thinking about taking her off life support," Jessie told me.

My heart plummeted. "Take her off life support? That's so horrible. I was hoping she'd be breathing on her own by now. I was really praying that she was going to make it," I said.

"Me too," Jessie said. "Well, anyway, Alan said he couldn't even think about taking her off life support yet. He said both he and his wife need more time," he replied.

"Yes, I can definitely believe that. It's all happening so fast, and it was so unexpected. I would want more time too. More time to pray for a miracle."

The miracle came exactly three days later. Alan Walker sat next to Bethany in her room in the intensive care unit, much as he had done each day since his wife went into cardiac arrest. He stroked her hair, caressed her cheek, and held her hand. "I don't want to live without you," he whispered softly.

Suddenly, Bethany's eyes popped open and focused on her husband. "What just happened to me?" she asked.

Thank you, Lord, for the priceless gift of life!

....

Over the next couple of years, I ran into Mrs. Walker in various places—biking around Pine Cove, shopping at the supermarket, and strolling on the boardwalk. I learned that she retired from her job and started her own catering business. Just the sight of her filled me with joy.

Thank you, Lord, for letting me bear witness to such a special miracle of life.

About 15 years had passed from the day our rescue squad responded to help Bethany. It was a beautiful October day, and my family and I were taking a walk on the boardwalk.

"Andrea, is that you?" a somewhat familiar voice asked.

I glanced up and saw a handsome, middle-aged gentleman with a bright smile. It was Alan Walker. "It's so wonderful to see you!" I exclaimed.

"Did you see Bethany?" he asked, pulling his baseball cap more firmly onto his head so it didn't inadvertently blow away with the wind.

"No, is she here with you?" I asked, my heart lifting with happiness.

Mr. Walker smiled and pointed toward the picnic tables at the pavilion about 25 feet away. "Come on over and say hello. It's been so long, and she'd love to see you," he said.

"I'd love to," I replied. Memories of that night came rushing back… the horror, the disappointment, and ultimately, the hope.

"Bethany, do you remember who this is?" Alan asked, coming up behind his wife and tapping her on the shoulder.

"Of course," she replied, a smile lighting up her face as we hugged.

"Bethany had a long, difficult recovery, but she's doing incredibly well now," Alan said, his eyes shining with pride.

"We're here watching my grandson play," Bethany said, pointing to a young boy who was frolicking on the beach. "That's Cole's son."

And that's when it hit me. I reflected on that night 15 years before when I had sent an urgent prayer for help up to heaven. Here we were, so many years later, and the answer to my prayers stood before me.

She's watching her young grandson play on the beach. A grandson that, if things had turned out differently that night, Bethany would never have met.

In that moment, I knew that a living miracle stood before me. The miracle of Bethany Walker.

About the Author

Andrea Jo Rodgers has been a volunteer EMT for 30 years and has responded to more than 7,000 first-aid and fire calls. She holds a clinical doctorate in physical therapy and has worked as a physical therapist in a trauma center for 20 years.

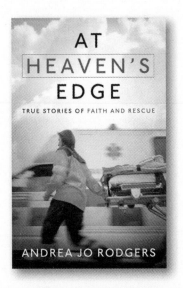

AT HEAVEN'S EDGE

TRUE STORIES OF FAITH AND RESCUE

ANDREA JO RODGERS

911...What Is Your Emergency?

Veteran EMT Andrea Rodgers has helped hundreds of people in their most vulnerable moments.

Some of the victims faced their mortality head-on and cried out to God for help. Many experienced fleeting but life-changing connections with their first responders. Often these crises became unexpected sources of inspiration.

Now Andrea shares brief, real-life stories of heroic courage in the face of fear. In times of intense suffering, she has repeatedly witnessed signs of God's quiet intervention and healing presence.

- A man is resuscitated after Andrea was able to repair a defibrillator—with her teeth!

- Several bystanders help rescue a young girl who is accidently buried alive in sand.

- Andrea also experienced some lighthearted moments, including the time she arrived at the scene of a crime only to find herself in the middle of a mystery dinner theater.

Experience miracles and life-and-death drama as you look at life from heaven's edge.

To learn more about Harvest House books and
to read sample chapters, visit our website:

www.harvesthousepublishers.com

HARVEST HOUSE PUBLISHERS
EUGENE, OREGON